OLDE YORKSHIRE PUNISHMENTS

Olde Yorkshire Punishments

Howard Peach

First published in 2008 by The History Press

Reprinted 2008, 2010

The History Press
The Mill, Brimscombe Port,
Stroud, Gloucestershire, GL5 2QG
www.thehistorypress.co.uk

© Howard Peach, 2008

The right of Howard Peach to be identified as the Author
of this work has been asserted in accordance with the
Copyrights, Designs and Patents Act 1988.

All rights reserved. No part of this book may be reprinted
or reproduced or utilised in any form or by any electronic,
mechanical or other means, now known or hereafter invented,
including photocopying and recording, or in any information
storage or retrieval system, without the permission in writing
from the Publishers.

British Library Cataloguing in Publication Data.
A catalogue record for this book is available from the British Library.

ISBN 978 0 7524 4661 5

Typesetting and origination by The History Press.
Printed in Great Britain

Contents

	Preface and Acknowledgements	6
1	Historical Background	7
2	Religious Penalties	16
3	Social Sanctions	31
4	Corporal Punishment	48
5	Prisons and Transportation	61
6	Capital Punishment	79
7	Chiding Children	99
8	Royal Reckonings	112
9	Changing Attitudes	124
	Select Bibliography	128

Preface and Acknowledgements

The germ of this book lay in a few casual jottings intended as the basis of a magazine article – until my notes became so copious that I realised I was staring at potential chapters!

None of us – archbishops, arch-criminals or ordinary citizens – needs reminding that crime and punishment are timeless matters, engaging often the emotions as well as the critical faculties. Rarely has there been a trade-off between severe punishment and falling crime rates, except for the temporary expedient of locking up blackguards. There is little evidence to support the idea that there ever was a golden age of minimal crime. Our own times could hardly be cited, as recently (2007) some prisoners have just been released to accommodate others – and Yorkshire has the sad reputation of being the worst county for burglaries and car crime.

Penalties and retributions have to be viewed in their historical and social context. National events, civil turmoil, economic hardship, new personalities often demand scapegoats as well as reformulations of the law. Parochial judgements by manorial courts or local justices have sometimes served to flavour national trends; many have considerable curiosity value. Time was when Kings and Queens had the power of life and death over their subjects, especially those with political ambitions. As one or two monarchs met a certain comeuppance here in Yorkshire, their fate adds an ironic perspective.

By highlighting some of the inexhaustible appeal of this vast subject from across all three Ridings, I have tried to show how Yorkshire has responded to issues of law and order. Some punishments have been unique and historic, like William the Conqueror's Harrying of the North and the Halifax gibbet. Other institutionalised sanctions (stocks, prisons, fines) will, of course, readily find echoes elsewhere. And there are plenty of examples of local courts and other authorities exacting unique and occasionally eccentric punishments.

I hope readers will find the following account useful and informative. May it lead to further exploration and reflection for us all.

For kindly providing illustrations, or for allowing me access to take photographs, I am most grateful to the following – Bankfield Museum, Halifax; Bar Convent, York; Black Swan Inn, Leyburn; Christopher Ketchell; Doncaster Library; Halifax Library; HM Prison, Armley; HM Prison, Hull; Humberside Police; Hull City Archives; Hull Museums; Langbaurgh on Tees Borough Council; Leeds Central Library; the Marquess of Salisbury; National Coal Mining Museum, Wakefield; National Society for the Prevention of Cruelty to Children; North Yorkshire Police; Punch Ltd.; Ripon Museums; Rotunda Museum, Scarborough; Ryedale Folk Museum; Selby Library; Wakefield Museum; *Whitby Gazette*; Whitby Literary and Philosophical Society; York Central Library; York City Art Gallery; York Museums; Yorkshire Archaeological Society.

chapter one

Historical Background

The Romans had a relatively advanced system of law in which plaintiffs and defendants met in local magistrates' courts. York (Eboracum) had a basilica for courts of law, while at Aldborough (Isurium Brigantum) an aristocratic local (ie native Brigantian) council ran the judicial system. Justice, often harsh, was enforced with full state backing.

During Saxon times territorial hundred courts developed with folk moots led by a bailiff. Crime was held to be 'against the peace' of the community. Adult freemen in groups of ten (tythingmen) were answerable for one another's behaviour. This so-called View of Frankpledge was continued into Norman times. The office of shire reeve (sheriff) also developed during this period. He was empowered to call up a local militia to put down serious challenges to public order. Punishments included stocks and the pillory, and, especially for runaway servants, whipping and branding. At Otley a quagmire was traditionally used to drown female thieves, though with what judicial authority is unknown.

Danish wapentakes (amalgamations of hundreds) raised soldiers, levied taxes and maintained law and order. Wetwang in the East Riding had a Viking name, Vertvanger, meaning 'place of justice'. A later Viking punishment was 'Ordeal by Fire', taking place in churches, like an earlier Ripon Minster. Watched by a congregation, the accused had to carry a hot metal rod for nine paces. If after three days binding the wound showed signs of healing, innocence was declared. In 1215, however, the Church decided that ordeals were superstitious and priests were forbidden to take part.

The Normans used the county as an administrative unit with the sheriff as Crown deputy. In later times his duties included attending assize judges, issuing and executing writs, custody arrangements and examining accused persons in preparation for court appearances. Sometimes organised representations were made to the sheriff by groups acting for accused persons. Thus, in 1293, twelve 'good men and true' from Wistow, near Selby, met in York to plead for the life of John Thorp, who had slain William Belle of Gateforth in alleged self-defence, not 'malice and hatred'.

From 1166 circuit justices met in county court sessions at York Castle. Their concern was more serious offences referred to them by local wapentake courts or the sheriff.

The Statute of Winchester in 1285 confirmed localities' responsibility for law and order. Towns had to appoint constables for 'watch and ward', i.e. night and day patrol. Under 'hue and cry', persons seeking to make an arrest could call for immediate help; and under the Assize of Arms fifteen to sixty-year-old men could be issued with weapons to keep the peace. Executive high constables in each hundred were to conduct inspections. Over succeeding centuries they gradually became collectors of fines.

Lords of the manor held two types of manorial court – the court baron, dealing with 'stones, bounds and stakes' (ie their own property, services and duties); and the court leet, concerned with day-to-day matters like trespass, straying animals, street refuse, market tolls and law and order.

These proved to be durable institutions. On 19 November 1657 the Ilkley Court Leet fined William Harrison of Wheatley the sum of 10s for causing an affray and drawing blood from Christopher Laycock. On 9 October 1663 the twelve members of the jury of the 'Court of the Rectory Manor of Patrington' (ER) fined James Addam 6d for not giving the proper weight of bread; James Mattock was fined 4d for leaving manure in the street, and Edward Barnard had to pay 4d for leaving a ditch undug. The lord of manor was responsible for investigating crimes, property or public order offences and for meting out justice, including fines, corporal punishment – even hanging. Until it achieved borough status in 1847, Bradford dispensed justice through its manorial court leet and baron, exercising jurisdiction over markets, weights and measures etc.

Traditionally, the court leet, under the lord's steward, appointed a constable to serve for a year. Carrying a staff as symbol of authority, this generally reluctant official reported offenders to the manor court, and where necessary, the quarter sessions. In Shakespeare's *Much Ado About Nothing* he was satirised in the character of Dogberry.

Originally, at least, he was unpaid, unwilling, untrained – and unfortunate. His unremitting duties amounted to social drudgery. Moreover, he attracted additional duties: maintaining the stocks and pillory; attending to pumps and wells, pinfolds and beacons and collecting rates and taxes. From 1591 he was liable to assist churchwardens in ensuring church attendance. In sixteenth-century Harrogate the constable also supervised the cutting of peat for fuel and the chopping of evergreens for feeding farm animals. Recognition of his functions brought fees and gratuities. In seventeenth-century Cherry Burton (ER) he received 2s for the arrest of every 'rogue' (vagrant), but was himself fined by his JP for any lapse of duty. Neighbours neglecting to help were also penalised. In 1607 Richard Seamer was presented to the Yarm Quarter Sessions for failing to assist constable John Robinson in the apprehension of certain vagabonds. Some escort duties were onerous. John Lyon, constable at Seamer in the early nineteenth century, had to lock up serious offenders overnight, then walk, or otherwise convey them, to York Castle for trial.

Drawn mainly from the ranks of tradesmen, craftsmen and journeymen – not from the professions, nor publicans, cripples, illiterates or 'persons without property' – most constables struggled to combine their two jobs. Henry Watkinson, constable of Ilkley in 1596, tried to continue his living also as a leather stamper. But some eventually profited: it was said that in 1760 Charles Campbell, constable and tea dealer, virtually ran the economy of Skipton.

Not every constable emerged from his year unscathed. In 1656 at Askrigg George Freer was attacked by eight men who then kidnapped his rate collectors. On 4 January 1643, as a diversion from their Civil War duties, a group of Roundheads from Broadfield 'arrested' Michael Green, constable of Emley, releasing him after two days. No wonder that some parishes, like early nineteenth-century Hawes, sometimes failed to recruit a suitable constable.

Not surprisingly, men chosen sometimes paid others to officiate for them. Nevertheless, the parish constable, as he became, until the nineteenth century remained the pivotal official in the day-to-day administration of law and order, answerable to his local justice of the peace.

A town required several constables. By the eighteenth-century Beverley had eighteen under the control of the mayor, recorder and JPs. Watch boxes remained on the streets of Hull until 1836 when Harry Lee, last of the greatcoated head constables, retired.

From 1361 the loose organisation of parish constables within each wapentake was augmented by justices of the peace, royal appointees responsible to the county sheriff. Recruited from the landowning class, they held quarter sessions in the market towns, their main responsibilities being to deal with more serious cases beyond the scope or reach of the manorial courts – such as murder and riot. They also fined constables for such neglect as failing to remove vagrants, or allowing escapes.

Their role was extended in 1368 to wage regulations, and in Tudor times to the summary jurisdiction of petty sessions. From 1531 they were concerned also with Poor Law and workhouse regulation.

Considerable dignity attached to the historic office of the Ripon wakeman, a title of Saxon origin. Originally accountable to the Archbishop of York for keeping watch from curfew to dawn, the wakeman blew his horn at 9 p.m. before shutting the town gates. Assisted by four constables, he was empowered to arrest strangers or malingerers met during the hours of darkness. Householders who had paid 2d a year for each door in their homes were eligible for compensation against burglars. Believed to have begun in 1285 'to abate the power of felons', the system lasted until 1604 when James I's charter granted local government to a mayor and corporation. Hugh Ripley, the last wakeman became first mayor and chief magistrate, chosen from twelve aldermen. Night watchmen continued to serve Ripon until 1875.

Inscribed boldly over the stonework of the Town Hall is the legend 'Except Ye Lord keep ye Cittie Ye Wakeman waketh in vain'. At 9 p.m. every evening the hornblower, dressed in eighteenth-century costume, still blows his horn at each corner of the market-place obelisk, and in front of the nearby Wakeman's House.

Elsewhere, many burgesses sought to cast off irksome manorial dues and services, wanting their own markets and court – privileges to be gained through royal or archiepiscopal charters. As early as 1127 Archbishop Thurstan conceded a charter to Beverley, which in return for annual payments granted the right to establish guilds and make bylaws, free from tolls and interference. A further charter of 1359 empowered twelve keepers (governors) to be responsible for punishing wrongdoers; and by a charter of incorporation of 1573 the town became entitled to a council of thirteen, including the mayor, and the right to its own system of courts, prisons, recorders and policing arrangements.

Ripon Town Hall.

Wakeman's House.

Some towns – like fifteenth-century Beverley and Ripon – became special liberties with their own JPs. York and Hull were governed by merchant aristocracies represented by a mayor, aldermen, council and an elected sheriff. Some towns, like Knaresborough, developed a variety of courts. The sheriff's tourn of the honour court, a grand court leet, was obligatory for all tenants at Easter and Michaelmas, and lasted up to the nineteenth century. The Wednesday customary court, held every three months in the castle, dealt with trespass, assault, fence breaking and other minor felonies. Between times the borough court sat on alternate Mondays in the toll booth (on the site of the present Town Hall) which has cells for overnight prisioners.

Local courts have been held in some curious places, including pubs such as the Bingley Arms, Church Lane, Bardsey, near Leeds, reputedly amongst our oldest hostelries. A pillory stood conveniently opposite the church. Birstall's Black Bull, near Batley, had an upper room with a built-in dock and magistrates' box.

Ecclesiastical courts exercised vast influence. From Howden's Moot Hall the Bishop of Durham dispensed justice up to and including the death penalty. At Selby the abbot's steward directed justice within the town. At Bridlington the prior, as lord of the manor, until 1537 held his court leet at the Bayle, exercising jurisdiction over commercial life including the Assize of Bread and Ale for the regulation of markets and fairs.

Thus across Yorkshire there developed a variety of local authorities with powers for maintaining the King's peace. From 1539 the establishment of the King's Council of the North confirmed York as the regional judicial centre. Set in King's Manor, it lasted till 1641. In general the supreme figurehead, a Crown representative, was the lord-lieutenant, one for each Riding by 1760. His original roles were to co-ordinate the militia, to liaise with sheriffs and keep records of county sessions, and to serve as head of the magistracy, recommending and supervising JPs.

Eighteenth-century courtroom, Guildhall, Beverley.

This Tudor church courthouse, Ripon, was the archbishop's manor court until the seventeenth century when it became the Liberty Gaol for felons, especially debtors.

Justices allowed themselves considerable discretion. In Victorian times some petty sessions were held in the home of the local magistrate, to which accused persons were brought. Henry Jubb JP of Moorgate, Rotherham occasionally dismissed a drunk and disorderly case if the singer agreed to join the church choir!

Many local courts lingered on for decades after being overtaken by changes in national administration. Ilkley's courts baron and leet provided a basis for administration until 1893, while the Howden Halimot enjoyed its jurisdiction until the Law and Property Act (1925). An interesting survival is the Danby Court Leet which oversees Lord Downe's estate on the North Yorkshire moors, meeting in October in Danby Castle and imposing fines for local offences like misuse of land, straying animals and trespass. Common-right holders are fined 2d for unacceptable absences!

Before the eighteenth century custodial punishment was rare (except for houses of correction from Tudor times for persistent vagrants).

The Industrial Revolution brought social turmoil to towns, with frequent breakdowns of law and order. The problem had been partly recognised by the Riot Act of 1714 which ordered the dispersal of a crowd following due reading by a magistrate. By the late eighteenth century the question of crowd control was showing the serious inadequacies of urban policing. Elderly night watchmen bearing lanterns and rattles were no match for determined villains. Halifax could call on but two constables, two deputies and a night watchman. A single set of handcuffs, or even the 'snitcher' favoured by some Yorkshire constables – a double length of rawhide attached to a wooden handle which could be twisted and pulled tight over an offender's wrists – was useless against a hostile mob. The militia had to be called out to deal with riots, particularly in West Riding towns after 1750.

Some infringements of the law brought disproportionately severe penalties for convicted persons. Some 200 offences carried the death penalty: stealing goods worth 40s from a house, or 5s from a shop, or anything from a person assaulted. So outrageous were some punishments that magistrates felt obliged to undervalue stolen goods so as to limit the strict applications of the law. It took a Lancashire cotton manufacturer's son, Sir Robert Peel, as home secretary, to introduce in 1823 bills for the abolition of hanging in respect of over 100 crimes.

But for many ordinary citizens, prosecutions were too few and often feebly pursued. The proliferation of unresolved crime saw a mushrooming of self-help groups, such as the Wakefield Society for Prosecuting Felons, 1786, assisting the constable with burglaries, arson, rustling and 'cutting of tenters or taking wool out of yards'. A similar group was started in Beverley two years later. At Heptonstall a Prosecution Society begun in 1816 survived until 1909, bringing private actions when the local constabulary seemed inert.

Ideas grew for a rates-assisted professional force. But powerful voices argued against mobilising illiterate workers to uphold the law: to arm the poorest, as the clerk of the peace at Wakefield pointed out at the time of the Luddite mill-breaking (1812-14), would be disastrous. There were fears that such a militia might be partial towards a popular uprising, and might not obey orders.

However, the success of the organised Bow Street Runners in London reduced street crime, and in 1829 Peel established the Metropolitan Police Force with agreed rules of professional conduct. The discredited watch was abolished and seventeen districts were provided with a hierarchy of officers ranging from superintendent to 'bobbies' or 'peelers'.

Progress in Yorkshire was uneven. Sheffield had been quick to see the advantages of a full-time force, appointing in 1818 a surveyor and deputy, with five sergeants, sixteen day policemen and fifty-six night watchmen, all in resplendent blue uniforms. From 1828 at Doncaster Thomas Tyme, gaoler, doubled as a police officer at 100 guineas a year, with additional help.

£3 REWARD.

WHEREAS some evil-disposed person or persons did, on the Night of SATURDAY, the 28th instant,

STEAL AND TAKE AWAY A REVERSIBLE OVER-COAT

The Property of Mr. ROBERT ENGLAND, out of the Yard adjoining the Shop occupied by the said Robert England, in Snaith, in the West-Riding of Yorkshire.

Notice is hereby given,

That any person or persons who may give such information as shall lead to the conviction of the Offender or Offenders shall, on such conviction, receive a Reward of TWO POUNDS from the "SNAITH ASSOCIATION FOR THE PROSECUTION OF FELONS," and a further Reward of ONE POUND from the said ROBERT ENGLAND; which Rewards shall be apportioned to such person or persons, and in such manner, as the said Association or any Committee thereof shall think proper.

EDWARD E. CLARK,

Snaith, 30th Oct., 1854.   Solicitor to the said Association.

A notice for the Snaith Association for the Prosecution of Felons. (courtesy of Doncaster Library)

During the 1820s Keighley's Poor Law officials, health officers and night watchmen were augmented by salaried constables.

Impetus to the establishment by watch committees of salaried officials was given by the Municipal Corporation Act of 1835. A Royal Commission of 1836 confirmed that the old routine of 'watch and ward' was ineffective. In the same year Beverley had appointed new constabulary ranks based on the Metropolitan model, and Hull under Andrew McManus had four inspectors, two assistant inspectors, nine sergeants, and seventy-one constables. In Leeds there was continuity, with the superintendent of the night watch appointed as head constable, and four colleagues continuing as inspectors.

Further to the 1839 Rural Constabulary Act local stations were built in the smaller towns, mostly with lock-up provision. Yet there was resistance. At Yeadon in 1849 plans to hire a constable at 15s a week were withdrawn as unnecessary, a threat to customary liberties and certain to add to the burden of existing rates for the poor, the highways, the Church…

But the tide was irresistible. By the County and Borough Police Act of 1856, it became mandatory for committees and JPs to organise professional constabularies. Ex-military men were appointed as chief constables: Col. Charles Augustus Cobbe for the West Riding, Capt. Thomas Hill for the North Riding, and Lt-Col. Bernard Granville-Layard for the East Riding. Divisions were run on military lines and petty sessions organised in appropriate townships.

Recruits had to be literate and not less than 5ft 7in in height. Early uniforms consisted of a frock-coat tunic, white trousers, greatcoat, cape and a 'pork-pie' hat. Helmets came in during the 1860s.

For most recruits there was only immediate on-the-job training. For many years reports were propagated of offences by the new breed of officers. Drink was a widespread problem. Respect had to be earned. In 1857 an officious bobby was beaten and paraded naked around the Wibsey (Bradford) alehouses by a jeering mob. The Otley Conduct Book revealed that in July 1875 one constable was fined 10s for using 'insubordinate language and threatening to knock his sergeant's eyes up'. Five years later, for the offence of allowing an inebriated prisoner to enter a Guiseley inn, an officer was reduced to the rank of third-class constable.

Some were too zealous. In 1891 a Bridlington constable was unhappily discovered up a ladder at midnight, peering into a bedroom window! He was subsequently placed on a different ladder – at the foot of a list of second-class constables – and removed to another station.

More serious disturbances showed that even an experienced force sometimes seemed but 'a thin blue line' stretched to breaking point. Disturbances at Lord Masham's Ackton Hall Colliery in 1893 resulted in strikes, lockouts and a mass picket. After scuffles, and with troops of the South Staffordshire Regiment on standby, the Riot Act was read; rifles were raised and two workers were shot dead. In the history of West Riding folklore the Featherstone Massacre remains an inglorious and bitter milestone.

Over time, views on behaviour and sanctions change, especially with shifts in authority. It will be appropriate to turn next to religiously inspired developments.

An early Victorian policeman, West Riding – at entrance to Ripon Police Museum.

Selby Police Force, 1890. (courtesy of Selby Library)

Bobbies' batons. (courtesy of Ryedale Folk Museum)

chapter two

Religious Penalties

Church courts

The influence of the medieval church was pervasive, especially through the various institutions of the Archbishops of York. Archbishop Thurstan (1114 – 1128) held courts in such towns as Otley, Patrington, Sherburn, Ripon and Beverley using the customary sanctions of stocks, pillory, fines, prison – even hanging.

At Ripon the canons' court treated offences like Sabbath breaking, defamation and matrimonial disputes. Borough courts, presided over by the archbishop's steward, settled such secular matters as tolls and markets, vagrancy and sanitation. Local consistory courts dealt with tithes, moral offences, doctrine, pew rights, brawling on Church premises, blasphemy, abuse of churchwardens… all commonly punished by fines and ritual penances (of which more later). Refusals to comply could bring excommunication – i.e. exclusion from divine worship and participation in the sacraments.

Further control over parishioners' lives was exercised through archdeacons' visitations when churchwardens presented lists of blasphemers, adulterers, scolds, drunkards, cohabiters, unlicensed schoolmasters, midwives and surgeons. Each was obliged to do penance, pay fines or otherwise redeem sins on pain of excommunication. The general climate of belief certainly induced many to ponder their plight. Fears were stoked by church-rood paintings of hellfire punishments on Judgement Day. Frescoes like those rediscovered in St Peter and St Paul parish church, Pickering concentrated impressionable minds on the martyrdoms of John the Baptist, St Edmund and Thomas Becket, Archbishop of Canterbury, done to death at his own altar in 1170. The perpetrator-in-chief of this last wicked deed was Hugh de Morville, former constable of Knaresborough Castle (where he and his fellow conspirators sought sanctuary). Part of his penance was to build the church of St Thomas Becket at Hampsthwaite, Nidderdale.

Sometimes a church achieved peculiar or 'particular' status, like the court of Masham which had its own jurisdiction independent of the archbishop. Its seal shows an offender kneeling and awaiting a verdict.

Particularly dramatic were the public 'trials'. A historic trial by combat, in around 1260, lasted from dawn to sunset, St Mary's Abbey in York defeating the monks of Meaux (near Hull) over fishing rights on Hornsea Mere.

In the Saxon crypt of Ripon Cathedral, a woman accused of being unchaste could have been required to carry forward for nine paces a red-hot iron bar. If, after three days, the wound festered, she was declared guilty to suffer further punishment.

Unique medieval weeping cross, All Saints churchyard, Ripley (NR). The eight kneeholes around the base were for pilgrims or penitents.

Seal of the Peculier Court of Masham.

Abuses – In-house chastisements

Self-inflicted punishments were commonplace in Rievaulx, where monks scourged themselves with lengths of copper wire carrying lead weights. And raw nerves were touched by some penalties: in 1090, Benedict Abbot of Selby had two of his monks castrated for stealing silver. Accused of cruelty, he was forced to resign. A later abbot, Thomas de Whalley, refused to preach, rarely heard matins but from his bed, generally neglected his duties, enforced no discipline and was a serial fornicator. He was defrocked in 1262 (and again in 1280), banished and excommunicated.

In 1286 defaulting lay brothers at Newburgh Priory were whipped, confined and given extra duties. Nuns, too, were severely reprimanded, isolated, obliged to do penance and given humiliating tasks. One York legend tells of a nun walled up alive in St Leonard's Hospital, on the site of the present Theatre Royal, where the ghost of 'the grey lady' has allegedly been seen by actors and visitors.

Sanctuary

Rights of sanctuary were widely available, notably at Beverley and Ripon Minsters by grant of King Athelstan in AD 937. A criminal might seek protection of the Mother Church, but if the matter was not resolved within forty days he had to submit to banishment. Dressed in white robe or sackcloth he was escorted to a port and put aboard the first available ship. Restrictions were imposed by Henry VIII, and church sanctuary for criminals was abolished in 1623.

The 'frid stool', or 'sanctuary chair', Beverley Minster.

Benefit of Clergy

This was based on the Biblical text, 'Touch not mine anointed and do my prophets no harm' (I Chronicles 16:22). In time it came to apply to all who could read, on demand, the first verse of Psalm 51 – the so-called 'neck verse' (saving one's neck). As almost any illiterate could learn this by heart, the benefit was in contempt of common sense, as well as justice. The privilege fell into disuse, but was not abolished until 1827.

One cleric who failed to benefit for long was Roland Mewburne who, having knifed Robert Manfield at Wycliffe in 1482, claimed benefit and was granted a royal pardon. But the victim's brother organised a gang who mugged the priest, despatching him with a farm knife. The innumerable scandals and abuses of monastic institutions were contributory causes of Henry's decision to dissolve them.

Tithing troubles

Tithes, payment of one-tenth of their income in kind by tenant farmers, caused great resentment. John Milde, vicar of Masham and Kirkby Malzeard, was frequently involved in litigation. In 1552 he sued a parishioner for non-payment, and two years later appealed to the dean and chapter of York against the abbot and convent of Fountains Abbey, no less, for unpaid tithes. As a popular couplet showed –

> We've cheated parson, we'll cheat him again
> For why should vicar tak yan i' ten?

Tithes had long been a compensation for poor stipends. Of indifferent quality, too, were many of the goods earmarked for the parson. As Sydney Smith, vicar of Foston le Clay (near York) pointed out, the parson felt obliged to 'officiate in the cornfield' to ensure his tenths. Ironically and sadly, Sydney once made a little girl stand for hours in the middle of his lawn with a placard declaring 'thief' about her neck for raiding his orchard.

With the emergence of nonconformity, tithes were still more bitterly contested. Nicholas Raw of Feetham, Swaledale, a Quaker, was gaoled for four years at York Castle for refusing tithes to Tobias West, vicar of Grinton, in 1678. His religious stance doubtless contributed to the penalty. Punishments for repeated non-payment could result in excommunication, the fate of Nicholas Mewburn, a Stokesley weaver, in 1744 for failing to render his Easter tithes. The matter festered on until the Tithe Commutation Act of 1836 commuted tithes for money or rent charge, or in some cases, like Walkington (near Beverley) concessions of land.

Other secular matters

Some cases were heard within the shadow of the church. Occasionally porches were used as minor courts, e.g. at All Saints', Great Ayton during the thirteenth and fourteenth centuries. Stocks were generally close at hand, often in the churchyard itself, as at Burnsall. For centuries Keighley market, with customary provision for dealing with theft and short measures, was held on Church Green. At Beverley a short 'gate' (street) linked market and Minster where in 1578 Marmaduke Jeakell was fined 6s 8d for forestalling fish by selling it before the opening bell rang.

In York and elsewhere the craft guilds, with active church support, imposed penalties (loss of franchise, even imprisonment) for their members' anti-social actions. Butchers were forbidden to drop offal in the Ouse or in the street. Hull bricklayers were denied the alehouse, dice, cards or 'unthrifty games', with fines of 8d for each offence. Down to the nineteenth century the church's hand was clear in the drafting of apprenticeship indentures forbidding time-wasting leisure and enjoining sexual abstinence.

In fourteenth-century Beverley, craftsmen mounted the Corpus Christi play on the Thursday after Trinity Sunday, under penalty of a fine for default. In 1482 Henry Cooper, a weaver, was fined for not knowing his lines! Especially at York and Wakefield, the mystery plays provided a regular platform for portraying ideas of heaven, hell and divine punishment.

Reprisals against archbishops

Despite their privilege and power, some archbishops' political involvement brought severe penalties. Richard Scrope, Archbishop of York, supported the Mowbrays and Percys against Henry IV (Bolingbroke), accusing him of the murder of Richard II, and nailing an impeachment document to the door of Stokesley church. Scrope held protest meetings on Shipton Moor and raised an army of 20,000, encamped in the Forest of Galtres. A false parley was followed by his arrest and trial at Bishopthorpe. On 8 June 1405 the archbishop, clad in mocking purple, was lifted onto a carthorse, and led into a field where he requested the executioner to give him five blows in memory of the five sacred wounds of Christ. His head was mounted on the city walls.

After incurring the displeasure of Edward IV, George Neville was banished, in 1473, to a French prison. Thomas Wolsey, Henry VIII's lord chancellor, unable to deliver the papal annulment of the King's marriage to Catherine of Aragon, was stripped of all offices save that of nominal Archbishop of York. Four days before his official enthronement he was arrested on a charge of high treason, but died at Leicester Abbey en route to the Tower. Cardinal John Fisher, son of a Beverley merchant, was beheaded in 1535 on Tower Hill for refusing to swear to the new establishment. Archbishop Holgate was apprehended as a reformist, unsympathetic to

Archbishop Scrope.

Catholic Queen Mary's Mass and reconciliation with Rome. After spending eighteen months in the Tower of London he was released into retirement, dying in 1556.

Lesser clerics suffered too. John Dobson, vicar of Muston, near Filey, was hanged, drawn and quartered at York for having spoken well of the pope but ill of the King in an alehouse. In 1534 the Revd Richard Browne, found guilty of heresy, was forced to walk barefoot around Holy Trinity church, Hull, carrying a big bundle of sticks.

The short reign of her Catholic Majesty, Mary (1553-58), daughter of Catherine of Aragon, brought persecution, deprivations and death. Married priests were driven from their livings; Nicholas Sonley of Welburn, near Kirkham Priory, having wed Isabella Chapley was ordered not to consort with her. On the death of Mary and the accession of her half-sister, Elizabeth, in 1558, Protestantism returned. An Act of Supremacy required an oath by clergy and secular officials to acknowledge the Queen as supreme governor of Church and State.

Church attendance

This became compulsory on pain of a fine of 1s for every lapse – a situation that lasted for more than a century. Recusants, especially clergy, were vigorously harassed. John Bolton, a former canon of Warter Priory and in a living at Hilston, near Withernsea, was incarcerated in York Castle and later in the Hull Blockhouse, where he died.

Archbishop Edmund Grindal (1570-76) organised a thorough clearing of Roman vestments, ornaments, icons and service books. At his court in 1571 the curate of Askrigg was fined 13s 4d (and the churchwardens 10s each) for not destroying Catholic images – which now had to be burned publicly on market days in, for example, Middleham and Richmond.

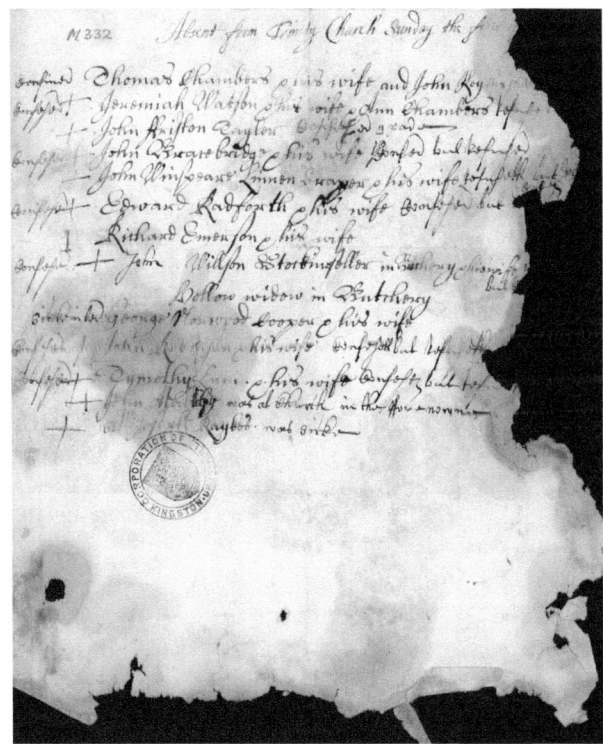

Holy Trinity church absentees, 1670.
(courtesy of Hull City Archives)

Priest holes

After the abortive Rising in the North, 1569 (see chapter eight) there was a further tightening of the laws against recusant priests, JPs issuing warrants for their arrest. Many went into hiding. Among the innumerable priest holes in Yorkshire is the Bingley Arms, Bardsey, known up to about 1780 as the Priests Inn, where the refuge was in a chimney. Dozens of priests were executed, including Francis Ingilby of Ripley, near Ripon.

More social control

With the accession of James I in 1603, the churches continued to exercise considerable social control. Parents failing to baptise infants, and parishioners caught playing cards in church, were fined. In 1625 the father of an illegitimate child had to pay 4d to Catterick church each Sunday until the youngster reached seven years. Downright abuse often brought punishment: at the mayor's court, York, in 1614, Thomas Nicholson, for sneering at sermons outside All Hallows church, for cursing worshippers and throwing snowballs at them, was sentenced to stand at the church door the following Sunday with a notice on his head *re* his 'opprobrious words'.

New World salvation

A less stringent official view of the religious Sunday had come with King James's *Book of Sports*, 1618 which had to be read in churches, permitting games, archery practice and even dancing after Divine service. Many priests took exception, among them the vicar of Rowley (near Beverley), Ezekiel Rogers, who refused to read the book to his congregation, an omission condoned for many years by Archbishop Matthew. When the latter was succeeded in 1632 by Richard Neile, warnings were issued. Rogers was called to York for not wearing a surplice, for omitting parts of the service and for not celebrating certain holy days. Finally this religious maverick assembled a large number of followers and left Hull to found a new Rowley in Massachusetts in 1638, just eighteen years after an Austerfield Man, William Bradford, had sailed with the *Mayflower*, becoming governor of Plymouth Colony until his death in 1657. Thus began the emigration of groups of worshippers, penalised in their Yorkshire homeland, to play influential and political roles in the colonisation of New England.

Civil War

There were many abuses of church property. Horses were deliberately kept in Ripon Cathedral, where medieval glass was shattered and wall monuments wrecked. Selby Abbey suffered the depredations of both armies. Cromwell's soldiers smashed the north transept windows, but it was the King's men who stabled their horses, set up a barracks and destroyed remaining Catholic images. York fortunately won an honourable surrender. Sir Thomas Fairfax insisted on total restraint for the Minster, and the city records also were preserved.

Many clergymen were humiliatingly punished. The Revd Robert Thornton was expelled from his Birkin living, near Pontefract, in 1646 by Parliamentary soldiers who tied him to a horse's tail, dragging him all the way to Cawood Castle. He survived, though badly bruised.

Inevitable too was the renewed Puritan purge on Sabbath breakers. Constables were now to levy 3s 4d for offences like bull-baiting, games or plays on Sunday. Non-payers were imprisoned or consigned to the stocks.

Yearnings for fuller religious and civil freedom were behind the emerging Quaker movement. A servant girl, Mary Fisher pointed the way dramatically in 1652 when she shouted at the vicar during a Selby Abbey service: 'Come down, tha painted beast, thou art but a hireling, and deludest the people with thy lies!' Even for a blunt Yorkshire lass, this was strong. She was imprisoned in York Castle and flogged for throwing a stool at a minister and otherwise 'declaring truth' in a Pontefract 'steeple house' (ie ordinary church).

'Steeple house' was a derogatory phrase cultivated by George Fox, founder of the Society of Friends, who visited York in 1651 during a tour of the Ridings. Refusing to pay church rent and tithes, he saw religious experience as a quiet meeting of friends receptive to the inward light of God without the pomp and ceremony of liturgy. Arrested during a visit to Scarborough in 1665, he refused to accept the magistrates' authority, keeping his hat on when hauled before them. He spent sixteen months in the town castle, where, as he complained in his journal, his room was open to wind and rain. His captors often threatened to hang him over a wall. After appealing to Charles II he was freed.

Discrimination

Other religious communities were penalised by discriminatory laws. The Corporation Act of 1661 sought to exclude nonconformist ministers from all boroughs. Under the Act of Uniformity of the following year, imposing a revised Book of Common Prayer, 123 Puritan clergy were driven from their Yorkshire parishes. Peter Clark, vicar of Kirby Underdale (ER) for the past fourteen years, was ejected, moving to Walkington where he established a successful boarding school.

Roman Catholics also suffered. The Test Act of 1673 required the taking of strict Church of England oaths, denying others public office, military careers or university education. Even the Duke of York (the future James II) was compelled to resign as high admiral.

But it was the execution of Catholic priests that provoked outrage. At Egton Bridge (NR), Father Nicholas Postgate conducted baptism and held services in the Old Mass House and had a hiding place at Ugthorpe Old Hall. Tradition has it that his betrayer, John Reeves, subsequently drowned himself at Littlebeck. After trial in York in 1679 Postgate was hanged, drawn and quartered, 'Martyr of the moors', at the age of eighty-one. A shrine to his memory stands in St Hedda's RC church, Egton Bridge.

Scarborough skirmishes

Noteworthy on a lighter side in 1688 were the local consequences of an interim Declaration of Indulgence allowing a measure of freedom to recusants, both Catholic and nonconformists. In Scarborough a Protestant minister, Noel Boteler, refused to read the Declaration publicly, whereupon the mayor belaboured him with a stick at the lectern. Incensed, another parishioner, Captain Ousley, rebuked Mayor Thomas Aislabie and had him tossed in a blanket. After various appeals to the new King William, the mayor was sacked and two bailiffs appointed.

Woollen shrouds

Another example of government fiat particularly affecting Yorkshire was an Act of 1678 insisting that all corpses should be buried in wool. The industry was in the doldrums at the time. Before the year was out, Margaret Marshall was dutifully buried at Myton upon Swale, 'in nothing but woollen only, according to ye tenour of ye late Act', with an affidavit sworn by her next of kin

Above: A priest being tortured in 'Scavenger's Daughter'. (courtesy of Bar Convent, York)

Left: Nicholas Postgate, a Catholic priest, was hanged, drawn and quartered in 1679 at the age of eighty-one.

before Sir Henry Stapylton JP. But transgressions were many. In 1692 at St Andrew's church, Grinton (NR) Adam Barker, a lead miner, was fined £5 for burying his daughter Ann in a linen shroud. The Act, evaded by those who could afford burials in richer cloths, fell into gradual disuse, but was not formally repealed until 1863.

Resurrection men

Time was when corpses attracted a different kind of attention – this time by body snatchers. During the 1820s and '30s York was plagued by their activities, the city being on the high road to Edinburgh, where newly interred bodies were in demand by medical students, £12 per cadaver being the going rate. In 1831 John Hodgson, solicitor's clerk, stole the corpse of Thomas Rothery from the Episcopal Chapel, Wortley. At Leeds Borough Sessions he was sentenced to six weeks in York Castle and bound over for two more years of good behaviour, supported by two sureties guaranteeing him at £50 each, plus £100 of his own. These extra penalties presumably arose from his professional connections, together with a refusal to implicate his medical associates.

Some churches like, St Robert's, Pannal, placed heavy stone slabs over new graves for several weeks so as to deter re-entry. A reminder of these times, built by the Feoffees family, is the watch-house near the gates of St Nicholas church, Upper Bradfield (near Sheffield), where vigil was kept from the middle of the eighteenth century.

Knawpers

While faithful dog owners slumbered through many a tedious sermon, the hounds played havoc up and down the aisles. Thus the need for a dog patrol, or dog whipper, arose. For hundreds of years churchwardens' accounts itemised payments – for example, for the year 1706 the whipper ('knawper') at Yeadon was paid 3s. Fortunately, by 1833, the year of William Brown's election to Ilkley All Saints church as dog whipper and sexton, the first part of his title appeared to be obsolescent.

Such was the problem with stray dogs in Hull and York that St Luke's Day, 18 October, was long relished as Dog Whipping Day, an organised orgy of violence resulting in the deaths of hundreds of dogs, and which survived up to about 1850.

Well known as York's shortest street is Whip-Ma-Whop-Ma Gate. Opinions are divided as to whether this curious name derived from felons speeded here en route to gaol, or whether it was once dog-whipping territory. Or did the name originate with an ancient bylaw (unrepealed, aver some citizens) permitting a husband to bring his drunk and disorderly wife here and publicly whip her sober?

Penances

Adultery was still harshly paraded. On four successive Sunday mornings in January 1766 James Beadnell did full penance before a watchful congregation in Stokesley Parish church. Barefoot, clad in a white sheet from shoulder to ankles, and carrying a white wand, he expressed contrition for adultery with Ann Andrews. Erring clergy could often expect leniency. Nine years later the Revd Cornelius Rickaby, found guilty of fornication with Ann Vickerman of Speeton (near Filey), duly confessed and had his penance commuted to a ten-guinea fine; the lady was required to do full penance in Bessingby church, Bridlington.

The watch-house, St Nicholas churchyard, Upper Bradfield.

Ancient York street: were felons once beaten here?

Defamation

This was similarly punished by the church courts. In 1711 David Hall of Skipton, critical of Anglican clergy, was excommunicated in the archdeacon's court for having preached repentance in the market place, and causing a disturbance. In 1815 William Hepworth, shoemaker, did penance in Wakefield parish church for defaming Elizabeth Blacketer, both living in the Cock and Swan Yard, Westgate. Gradually these public humiliations were replaced by fines, and from 1857 church courts were confined to church matters.

Mad Grim

An incumbent who fought strongly against the prevailing lethargy of his Haworth parish was William Grimshaw – or 'Mad Grim', as he came to be known.

In her *Life of Charlotte Brontë*, Elizabeth Gaskell may have exaggerated his flamboyant side, but it appears that by various stick-and-carrot approaches from 1742, he transformed the worshipping habits of his flock. In four years twelve communicants had risen to 1,200, and in 1755 the church had to be enlarged. It is famously told that during the singing of Psalm 119 – all 176 verses – he took the opportunity of hunting idlers in the churchyard, streets and alehouses and driving them through the open church door. His charisma attracted enthusiastic congregations. He challenged a gang of youths making themselves a nuisance, reproved them, took their names and commanded them to visit him for further chastisement. Before the Haworth Races, notorious for drunkenness and carnality, he prayed for rain; after a three-day downpour the event was never revived. He took to disguising himself, mingling with malefactors and revealing himself at the right moment. Yet he had his human side, commanding a blacksmith to shoe a horse on a Sunday when a distant midwife had to be brought in. Grimshaw regularly invited Wesleyan

William Grimshaw.

brethren to his pulpit. Hundreds squeezed into pews when John Wesley or George Whitfield was preaching (though on one occasion in 1748 Wesley and Grimshaw were attacked by a mob near the Lancashire border).

Not a physically robust man, he was outside in all weathers and died in 1763 at the age of fifty-five. The appellation 'Mad Grim' stuck during his incumbency, but later generations have remembered him as the Apostle of the North.

Mob violence

The ecumenical spirit was less evident at Pateley Bridge in 1752 when the vicar incited a mob against a Methodist preacher, Thomas Lee. The crowd beat him, rolling him into an open sewer before setting him on a horse and running him out of town.

Back at Haworth it was a donkey with its rider facing the wrong way that brought mayhem into the church for Patrick Brontë's predecessor in 1819. In the early weeks of his incumbency the Revd Samuel Redhead's manner irritated his congregation and it quickly showed in a noisy exodus with a clattering of clogs. The poor man, reviled, his cloth cursed in contempt, on one occasion fled to the comparative safety of the Black Bull in order to escape rough handling. Whereas Redhead lasted barely four weeks, the Revd Brontë officiated in Haworth for forty-one years – though he came to think it prudent to keep a loaded revolver by his bedside.

John Nelson: plaque in Ivygate, Bradford recalling opposition to early Methodists.

All these matters, however, were trivial compared to an earlier act of horrifying anti-Semitism recorded on a plaque at the foot of Clifford's Tower, York: 'On the night of Friday, 16th March 1190 some 150 Jews and Jewesses having sought protection in the Royal Castle from a mob incited by Richard Malebisse and others chose to die at each other's hands rather than renounce their faith'.

When the castle was set on fire the fathers cut the throats of their families, and in turn presented themselves to the knife of the rabbi. The few survivors were killed the following morning.

Victorian vigilance

Many sanctions familiar in medieval times were evident. It was still common for beadles and churchwardens to carry a cane to 'bray' irreverent youngsters. At Ripponden church, for example, attended by several local schools, boys attending matins were often prodded by the verger's wand. Village squires, paid obsequious deference, kept an admonitory eye from their dominant pew. Some pews are still in situ, as at Boynton, Hotham, Knapton St Edmund's and Tong St James, while St Peter's, Croft has the giant Milbank pew.

Tipsy worshippers could still qualify for a cooling-off period in the stocks, which were once quite usual outside churches. In 1860 a Cropton ploughman had his horses removed by incensed neighbours for daring to work on the Lord's Day. A royal proclamation still exhibited in Beverley Minster, dated 9 June 1860, ruled against any Sunday indulgence in dice or cards, whether in public or private houses; judges, JPs and sheriffs were to prosecute all found guilty of gaming or beer selling during the hours of divine service.

Clifford's Tower, York was used as a jail until 1684, when the roof was blown off.

Rose Carr. (courtesy of Christopher Ketchell collection)

In Methodist circles, too, there was scope for self-criticism. At Guisborough Quarterly Circuit Meetings in mid-century some members were named and shamed for moral backsliding. Some were removed from membership. Preachers, too, were occasionally moved on for immorality, inefficiency or insolvency. Yet Yorkshire Methodism remained an energising moral force and chapel attendance reached new heights in the closing years of the century: it was generally synonymous with cheerfulness, responsibility and education.

A redoubtable character moulded by Primitive Methodism was Rose Carr (1843-1913), a Hornsea carrier, local preacher and strong-arm merchant who had her own secular punishments for mockers who crossed her: one Hull City footballer found himself cooling down in a horse trough; two footpads trying to rob her had their heads banged together. Recalcitrant children were hushed by the threat of being confronted by Rose.

During the twentieth century the punitive elements in Church conduct were largely eliminated. For Christian believers, perhaps the Day of Judgment is enough. Some reminders persist: at midnight on Christmas Eve the Devil's Knell is rung – Black Tom – at Dewsbury All Saints church. It was instituted in the fifteenth century by Sir Thomas de Soothill as a penance for having killed a servant.

Down the centuries it was often hard to separate the influence of Church and State on local government. The religious dimension has continued to pervade so many aspects of life, as following chapters will further show.

chapter three

Social Sanctions

Common offences

Against the backdrop of history some offences seemed perennial – as in these fourteenth-century examples. In 1310 at Hutton-le-Hole, Walter of the Moor was fined five oxen and a stirk (a yearling ox or cow) for allowing his cattle to stray in the forest. For felling an ash tree on the land of Robert de Wyrunthorpe (Wrenthorpe, near Wakefield) in 1331, John Amabilla was fined 3d. John Milnthorpe and William Miller were apprehended in 1342 with many 'gryndlstones' in their possession, daringly excavated from their lord's demesne. At a court meeting at Rockley (Worsbrough) these items were confiscated and the men fined 4s for trespass, plus a further 4s 6d for making the finished products – grindstones. These they had hoped to use to grind their own corn instead of paying for the privilege of using his lordship's mill. In 1367 the Governors of Beverley, granted freedom of action by a recent charter, ordered that no carts shod with iron, and likely to damage surfaces, should be driven into the town, on pain of 12d for each offence.

Complaints about the state of the roads were to grow. In Tudor times road mending became a parish responsibility with the village constable striving to recruit unwilling labour. Guisborough was fined £40 in 1659 at the Helmsley Quarter Sessions for the poor condition of its highways; three years later the fine rose to £50.

More serious was the hazard of fire, especially amid closely built thatched cottages. Nun Monkton's court leet decreed in 1874 that no uncovered light should be carried from house to house on pain of fines up to £1 19s 11d.

Open coal shafts were a problem. In 1638 the lord of the manor of Baildon was prosecuted at Wakefield Sessions for leaving open shafts on the common.

Despite the stringent Game Laws, operating since the Norman Conquest in such royal forests as Galtres, poachers caused the authorities much trouble. In 1351 John le Woderward of Raskelf, forester, was blinded, and his tongue and fingers were cut off by ruthless men. Courts like the Easingwold Court of Verderers of Galtres regulated forest affairs, dealing with offences of venison (game) and vert (timber, underwood) and the illegal removal of peat from forest turbaries. There were many clerical offenders, like the Abbot of Whitby, fined 3s for taking a green oak from Goathland. And new outlaws were named, like Thomas the Stainton woodward, who had abused his trust by poaching.

Increases in penalties seemed to have little effect, and there were many confrontations. An Act of 1770 reiterated the range of punishments: three to six months in the house of correction for a first offence, up to twelve months for a second, plus a public whipping, and outlawry for a third. From 1816 hanging or transportation, sometimes commuted to military service, at least put offenders out of circulation. While the deterrent effect may be doubted, the use of iron traps

Spring trap. (courtesy of Ryedale Folk Museum)

An early nineteenth-century mantrap. (courtesy of the Black Swan inn, Leyburn)

during the difficult times following the Napoleonic Wars made impact enough for these devices to be made illegal in 1827.

Town life

While events like the murder of a policeman at Dodworth, Barnsley in 1886 by a poacher, James Murphy, who was hanged at York, inevitably make nine-day wonders, town life offered steadier excitement. Taverns licensed by JPs were expected to abide by clear standards. They were not to open during Sunday-service hours, and landlords were to keep an eye on unwed couples applying to occupy the same room. In 1616 the justices at Thirsk ordered Richard Hudson of Huton Bushnell, a forty-nine-year-old weaver, to be whipped through the town for leading 'players of Enterludes, vagabundes and sturdy beggars' who sang 'useless corrupt and filthy songs' at Easingwold. Examples were made of public figures who became indiscreet over their beer, as when Edmond Bateman, member of the council at Doncaster, was expelled in 1599 for disclosing council matters in common alehouses, and behaving 'unquietly and unorderly'. And many a local worthy must have cringed to be loudly named and shamed with the threat of court action by the town crier for neglecting to pay his rates.

Fairs and markets

Huge crowds were attracted by seasonal fairs, like Scarborough's, which under a charter of 1253 lasted from 15 August to Michaelmas. York's Lammas Fair, by contrast, began strictly at 3 p.m. on 31 July and closed at 3 p.m. on 2 August. This huge enterprise (foodstuffs, domestic items, farm stock, entertainers) was controlled by the archbishop's bailiff. Courts of Pie Powder (French *pieds poudreux*, 'court of dusty feet'), with juries recruited from traders, imposed summary sanctions, fines, stocks, pillory or even a whipping. Down to the nineteenth century Yorkshire fairs from Settle to Snaith opened with the bellman's proclamation from the market cross detailing the penalties, including imprisonment, that would befall anyone convicted of bringing weapons, causing disturbances, selling shoddy goods, issuing short measures, or selling foul ale (and so forth). Constables had to ensure that goods were sold only within prescribed precincts and stated times. During the later years of the eighteenth century the porter at Halifax Piece Hall stood to be fined 5s for admitting any customers for wools and worsteds before the ten o'clock bell, and anyone forestalling (selling prematurely) could be fined 1s. Severer penalties were known. For buying up fish coming into Stokesley market, Robert Sweeting of Knaresborough was fined one guinea and committed to the house of correction for two months. Elsewhere it was common practice to give away from the market cross underweight items or confiscated stock.

Bull-baiting

Until 1835 baiting was a legal requirement. Its justification lay, in part, in that meat was thought to taste better after a bull had been baited, that is, chained up and set upon by dogs. Butchers were penalised for defaults. On 25 October 1675 Kirkbymoorside Manor Court fined Robert Hardin 2s for failure to bait. A number of bull-rings remain – by Askrigg market cross and in Grassington Square (NR), for example.

Hunmanby Green lock-up.

Ancient Building

This building is the Old Village Lock-Up erected in 1834. It was in frequent use after the annual fairs & Martinmas which often ended in disorderly scenes. The Pinfold Built of Cobbles from the shore was used to impound straying Cattle.

Notice, Hunmanby Green lock-up.

Hirings

Other lively occasions were the seasonal hirings of farm workers – the 'Statties' – arising from past statutes, particularly the 1563 Statute of Artificers, dealing with conditions of appointment and wage assessments. These were set by JPs, with fines for infringements; by the eighteenth century, however, open bargaining in the market place had become the norm. Towns and times varied, but broadly in the North and West Ridings, hirings were around Michaelmas (late September) and the East Riding's (lasting well into the twentieth century) at Martinmas (November). A bargain reached constituted a contract, sealed by the farmer giving his new man a coin or 'fest'. Court cases resulting from broken contracts were mostly won by employers.

Hiring days were jollifications with old friends meeting, drinking, entertainment... but in adjacent yards and alleys some old scores were settled. Wagoners, for instance, once overfond of booting callow Tommy Owts (odd job lads) a few years earlier, might well meet their maturer match. And almost always with unruly scenes the old-time constables were helpless; the stattis hot-heads were left to their own rough justice.

Public disorder

Social events like the Doncaster race meetings showed increasingly how precariously balanced was law and order. In 1830 there were but six constables, helped at the races by twenty unpaid, untrained part-timers. Some units of West Riding yeomanry and dragoons were generally placed on close stand-by.

These 'special constables' were, in fact, troublemakers, recruited and kept drilling all day by the Whitby Superintendant to allow the 1864 parliamentary election to proceed smoothly! (courtesy of North Yorkshire Police)

A military presence was sometimes necessary at nineteenth-century elections, not least at Rotherham, where in 1865 violent opposition to the Tory candidate resulted in a reading of the Riot Act, and hussars smiting about them with the flat of their swords. At an election fifteen years later soldiers and police were slow to react; responsible townsfolk were assaulted, innocents 'nobbled' and a local editor arrested. This was an era when unpopular politicians were sometimes burnt in effigy.

From earlier centuries a general background of low living standards, low expectations during short lives, brutality and barbarism made violence endemic. During the Wars of the Roses King Henry VI had lamented (1457) that 'within our city of York… great slaughter, murder of our people and other mischiefs' had been carried out by robber gangs and 'overmighty subjects'. While few monarchs tolerated open opposition from their nobles, localised mayhem flared. Considering that the Percys had enjoyed a record of unpredictability in their loyalties to the Crown, it was ironic that Henry, 4th Earl of Northumberland, should be killed in 1489 during a Topcliffe riot while trying to collect taxes for Henry VII. His mangled remains (from death by scythe) were laid in Beverley Minster, not far from Grovehill, where in 1748 a mob critical of higher tolls killed a collector.

Not every Yorkshireman supported the wider social benefits brought by turnpikes and tolls. In 1753 a Leeds throng destroyed newly erected toll gates at Harewood. Soldiers were called in, eight rioters were killed and many more injured.

On 9 June 1757 John Wesley wrote in his diary:

> I rode over the mountains to Huddersfield… a wilder people I never saw in England… just ready to devour us… how intolerable a thing is the Gospel of Christ to them who are resolved to serve the Devil.

Five years later a hostile crowd hurled clods and stones at him while he was preaching in Holy Trinity church, Hull.

During the years 1780 to 1800 such was the disorder, drunkenness and wanton damage in the Wakefield/Dewsbury area that vigilante groups were set up for self-protection. Occasionally there was a resurgence of the Robin Hood spirit, as in 1799 when Martha Bray redistributed wheat stolen from a Golcar shop in the hope of feeding the poor. She was imprisoned for six months.

Even sympathisers like Frederich Engels (*Condition of the Working Classes in England*, 1844) conceded that the riotous behaviour of Sheffield youngsters created a new baseline. Repeated arson attacks on public property were hard to combat. Thieves' kitchens ('flash houses') were breeding grounds for crime in the wretched back-to-backs and squalid tenements of Leeds and Bradford, where up to the 1850s street warfare was commonplace. Sometimes there was a political dimension, as with the Chartist parade in Adelaide Street, Bradford on 29 May 1848 when police armed with cutlasses and staves confronted insurgents flailing brickbats and bludgeons. Dragoons were mobilised, many supporters were wounded and some later imprisoned at York.

Many doughty scrappers lived for glory and bloodlust. At Askrigg Hill Fair the custom was for a challenger to turn over the bullring outside the church; if another turned it back the fight was on. During the eighteenth century bare-knuckle bouts were eagerly followed about the Bradford area, on Fairweather Green or Eccleshill Moor. Village feuds were rife. Gangs of youths, stripped to the waist, fought pitched battles, all undisturbed by village constables, churchwardens or JPs.

Even within families there were combats to establish a fisticuffs hierarchy. At the Fountain Inn, Hawes in 1848 John and George Iveson struggled for mastery. George fell, hurt his head and died. His brother, tried for manslaughter, was acquitted, having spent four months in custody pending a court appearance.

A widespread form of intimidation was 'pitchering' – blocking the entry of outsiders to a village until they had dropped enough coins into a bucket (pitcher). Failure to comply meant a beating. In 1875 two Almondbury youths were fined for pitchering a Huddersfield lad coming courting on their territory.

Prudence

Victorian values, officially at least, demanded public reticence, especially in matters of dress and moral conformity. According to Scarborough bylaws of 1861, bathers were required to change in horse-drawn bathing machines, hired at sixpence per half hour. They had to keep at least 25yds away from the opposite sex – and women had to wear gowns. Inspectors could impose fines of up to 40s for failure to comply.

Smuggling

It was a way of life along the Yorkshire coast. To the hard-pressed revenue men it once seemed that entire villages – Flamborough, Robin Hood's Bay, Staithes, for example – were involved with the illegal transfer of brandy, wines, tobacco, tea, china etc. Such was the maze of doors, secret cupboards and passages in the Bay that contraband could pass from sea level to cliff top without ever seeing daylight – or so it was claimed.

Penalties were severe – a statutory fine of £100 and gaol, or possibly five years in the navy under the discipline of the lash. Additional punishments from 1736 were flogging, hard labour or transportation for resisting arrest, and death for using arms or wounding. Receivers, too, were penalised; £10 for each item from 1779, and the suppliers £50. But smugglers still took the risks.

There was also an illegal export trade. In 1700 John Rickaby, a Bridlington maltster, was sent to York Castle for shipping malt to Rotterdam, failing to pay duty of 1s per bushel. He was released after three years, having 'learnt his follys severelie'.

Robin Lythe's Hole: smugglers' retreat.

From this period stem many legends. During a tremendous thunderstorm in 1732 the Hornsea parish clerk was handling kegs in the church crypt. So furiously did the winds rage that the poor man, believing divine retribution was upon him, suffered a fit from which he never recovered. Another parish church in receipt of smuggled goods was at Marske-by-the-Sea where the sexton, William Stainton, hid away booty. In an unknown grave in the churchyard lies Will Watch, killed in a fight with the revenue men and buried at midnight.

In 1779 Richard Curtis of Staithes was brought to court in York for killing a dragoon by beating him with a stick. As the surgeon's evidence was inconclusive, Curtis was found not guilty on the capital charge, but as a smuggler was obliged by the judge to enter His Majesty's sea service by way of gaining a proper job!

It is claimed that at the Saltersgate Inn, on the A169 Pickering-Whitby road, the fire has never gone out since 1796; under the hearthstone was buried a customs man murdered by smugglers, and as long as the fire is maintained neither his ghost nor the Devil will appear!

At Saltburn it took decades for the 'Smuggler King', John Andrews, landlord of the Ship Inn, to receive his proper dues. Despite heavy involvement in smuggling he became captain of the local militia and master of foxhounds. Not until 1827 was he caught and sentenced, finishing up in York Debtors Prison after being unable to pay the fine of £100,000. Luckily for him, after two years his release was bought by influential friends.

Two developments signalled the end of the smuggling era – the appointment from the 1820s of large numbers of professional coastguards, tough, resolute and well armed, and progressive tax reforms, so that smuggling profits were much reduced and the risks calculated as too high.

Saltersgate hearth.

Smuggling prompted another social sanction – ostracism. Families of customs men were unwelcome. They met blank stares, threatening letters, abuse. Their children were picked on.

New arrivals anywhere have been regarded with a certain Yorkshire reserve, until acceptance has been earned. Misfits have been made sharply aware of their shortcomings. Local adulterers have found their houses linked by painted lines. Blackguards have had piles of rubbish dumped under their windows, or tubs of urine emptied by their doors.

Plague

In times of plague some form of temporary apartheid made sense. During the Black Death of 1348, York victims were confined to their homes, the red letter x marking their doors. A persistent legend tells of a young girl, believed by her family to be infected, who was bricked into an upper room – the ultimate sanction in desperate circumstances.

'The village of Shelf is dead,' declared an entry of 7 January 1350 in the Wakefield Court Rolls. Such a wiping out of whole communities was sometimes seen as the wrath of God, as in Old Testament times.

During the York outbreak of 1631, four men who dug up infected garments were put in the stocks and whipped. A spurrier, asked by the constable how his family was, confirmed that all were healthy, but the cat was sick – which amiable repartee earned him a spell in prison and a fine of 10s.

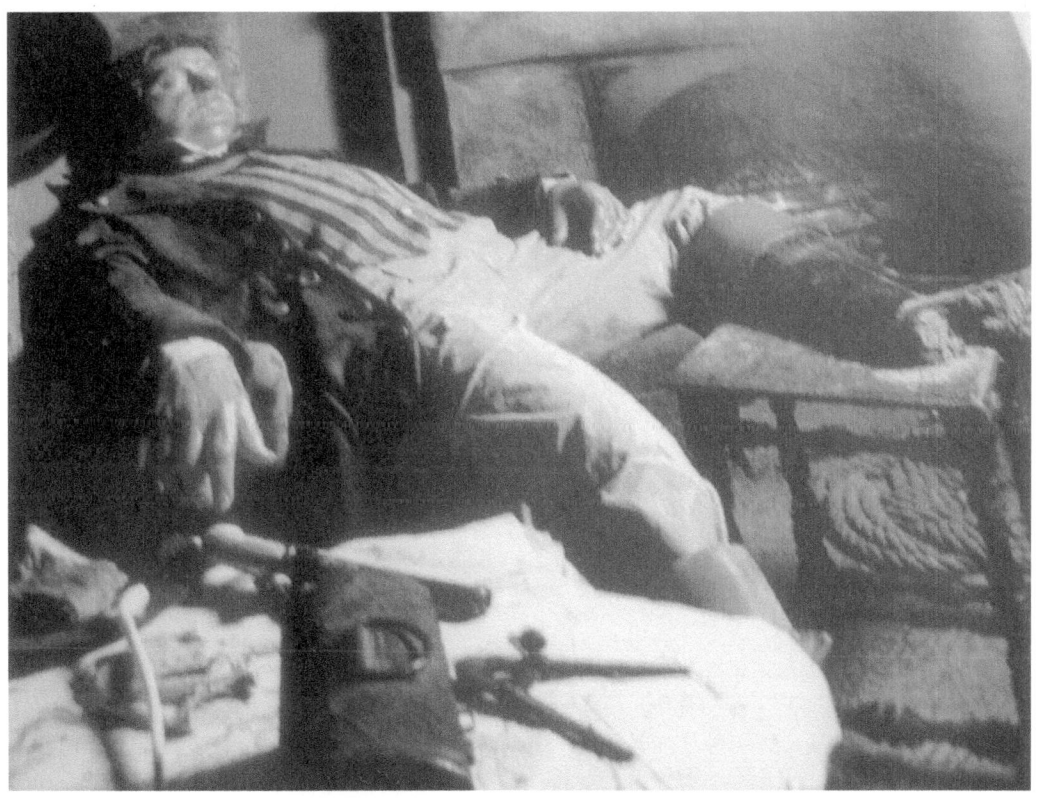

John Andrews. (courtesy of Langbaurgh on Tees Borough Council)

In August 1645 watchmen at Micklegate Bar were put on oath to scrutinise all entrants. Newcomers had to furnish passes certifying that they came from safe places and were not infected. In no circumstances were garments, bedding or cloth packs to enter – nor beggars, nor women pretending to be soldiers' wives. Twenty years later West Riding JPs instructed their constables to set up 'watch and ward' to guard against a still more serious, and historic, outbreak. All carriers from London were banned.

Stangs and effigies

Widespread in Yorkshire during the eighteenth and nineteenth centuries was 'Riding the Stang' to punish wife beaters or adulterers. The stang, or stee, was a ladder on which was mounted an effigy of the sinner. Propped up in a cart, it was pushed to the matrimonial home where a growing crowd created 'rough music' with pots, pans, saucepans and the like. At intervals the stang gaffer intoned a few lines of doggerel, denouncing the offender. For three nights this performance was repeated; the effigy was then burnt. Stangs ridden in the later years of Queen Victoria's reign included Lindley (1870), with a crowd estimated at 400; Lockwood (1876); Northallerton (1877); Hedon (1889); Guisborouigh (1891) and West Scrafton (1901). Magistrates and police turned a blind eye. Perhaps they had confidence in the efficacy of a public sanction drawing so much support.

During the early years of the nineteenth century there were extraordinary protests against Parson Cann of Mexborough, who was often drunk. A donkey was brought into church and urged up the pulpit steps, and the cleric retreated, followed by cans, noise, abuse and missiles. Outside, his effigy was burnt.

In 1865 Matron Levers of the Tadcaster Workhouse was accused of drinking, neglect and ill-treatment. After her effigy was paraded and burnt she took the hint and left. A grittier character, though, was Edgar Breffit, owner of the Aire and Calder glassworks at Ryebread. He remained undeterred both by his effigy being burnt and thrown in the river, and the eighteen-week strike which followed against his decision to cut wages.

Women's woes

Historically, there had been little doubt about women's inferior status. As 'chattels' they suffered many disabilities: few could sue for divorce; sexual sins required greater atonement; and a wife killing her husband was traditionally guilty of 'petty treason', somehow seen as more heinous than murder – though she could, admittedly, hope to avoid the gallows if she were pregnant.

Some wives were sold. In 1806 George Gowthorpe of Patrington led his wife into Hull market place with a halter round her neck, as if she were an animal. He left alone and twenty guineas richer. At Emley Cross in 1826 John Turton sold his wife Mary for 5s to William Kaye of Scisset. Incredibly, after her buyer's death she returned to Turton for another thirty years.

Witches

Nowhere was the persecution of women more obvious than in the treatment of witches. Many of our forebears were driven by irrational fears that virtually became articles of belief. A fundamentalist approach to the Old Testament underpinned these prejudices, in such categorical statements as 'Thou shalt not suffer a witch to live' (Exodus XXII, v.18). Popular superstition was bolstered by an Elizabethan law of 1563 making death caused by witchcraft a capital offence. One of the first actions of the new Stuart King, James I, was to publish a *Daemonology* justifying death for witchcraft. An Act of the same year, 1603, declared that a first offence for fortune-telling merited prison, and the second execution. 'Sorcery, charm or enchantment' also would be severely punished.

Retributions speedily followed. In 1604 Jennet Wressle and Mary Holland were hanged in Hull. The York hangman accounted for six unfortunates in 1622. Witch tests amounted to torture. With the 'swimming of witches', thumbs and big toes were cross-bound, and thus handicapped the poor woman was flung into pond or mere. If she floated she was deemed guilty. If she sank, and presumed innocent, she had to be retrieved before drowning. Sometimes it was too late, as with Meg Collert, ducked and drowned, 1719, in Iburndale Beck, Sleights.

Pin-sticking was accusatory and painful. The pin tested the body for a wart, a Devil's Mark, an extra pap: any minor scar would serve as proof. Normally down-to-earth Yorkshiremen believed what they chose. In 1699 Susan Ambler suffered a whipping and the ducking stool at Stokesley, accused of casting a spell on Adam Clark's sheep, which had produced only forty lambs, nine of them black.

Reasonable acquittals were not unknown. There were calls for the Wise Woman of Wakefield, Jennet Benton, to be put to the test over a right-of-way dispute with a neighbour, Richard Jackson. His run of bad luck caused hallucinations, his wife going deaf, and an invasion of poltergeists. Jackson went to court in 1656 but lost.

There were some male prosecutions. In 1677 Michael Woodhouse, a Wadsley tailor, admitting to sorcery, was sent to York Gaol. Other showmen emerged, including John Wrightson, the Wise Man of Stokesley, who, in the early nineteenth century, claiming to be the seventh son of a seventh son, made a precarious living by fortune telling, identifying thieves, prescribing nostrums, etc. By this time he was safe: the witchcraft laws had been swept away in 1735.

A witchpost to fend off the evil eye. (courtesy of Ryedale Folk Museum)

Tudor picture of witchcraft.

Bastardy

Parochial concern at pregnant but unmarried women had a financial bias. In many localities, like the honour of Knaresborough, single mothers were not tolerated lightly. The constable directed them back whence they came. Girls caught out, and lacking understanding at home, were obliged to seek shelter in a house of correction, or a workhouse – a situation not unfamiliar in the recollections of our oldest generation today.

Men were given the choice of marrying the mother, or being whipped on a succession of market days and paying maintenance. A minister of Rastrick church had to do penance for an illicit paternity. In 1581 Midgley overseers, intent on avoiding bastardy costs, actually gave Sarah Hargreaves the sum of £2 9s 4d towards her wedding expenses.

Tudor poverty and penalties

In Tudor times, against a background of suppressed monasteries and sheep enclosures putting men out of work, punishments most savage were aimed at vagrants. Most parishes whipped them back to their birthplace, 'cripple carts' carrying the infirm. Henry VIII ordered that for a second offence the gristle of the right ear should be cut off; and hanging could follow a third offence. Fortunately this law was but sketchily implemented, but from 1547 some vagrants were branded on the forehead. The longer term outcome was the establishment of houses of correction for the setting on to work (in wool, flax, hemp and iron, amongst others) of paupers and idle beggars.

By the Poor Law of 1601 every parish was made responsible for its poor. The burden of administration fell on elected overseers and churchwardens, who tried to keep their levy as low as possible. Strangers were unwelcome at the poor-house door. Redomiciling paupers led to ill feeling. In the East Riding when Beeford complained of its high rate, local JPs ordered

Dunnington and Lissett to help out. A further tightening of the law was made with the Settlement Act of 1662, whereby newcomers could be removed if they occupied a tenement worth less than £10 a year. Temporary permits, as for harvest, were allowed only if the parish of origin had agreed in writing to take them back. In practice, able-bodied skilled workers (such as ex-Derbyshire lead miners) were generally welcome.

Workhouses

It was the Spartan regime of the workhouse that haunted the folk memory: early rising, unappetising food eaten in silence, locked doors, pauper badges, with whippings and hard labour for backsliders. These were sometimes the realities of institutional life – though many outside had staple diets little better than porridge and oatcakes. Meals could be lost for defective table manners. 'Disorderly acts' (noise, neglect, card playing on Sundays) might be punished by a diet of bread and potatoes for forty-eight hours. 'Refractory behaviour' (abuse, drunkenness, violence) brought confinement on a bread diet for two days.

The minutes of the Halifax Workhouse confirm that during the seventeenth century it was a dumping ground for misfits – vagrants, scolds, felons, trespassers. In return for 'carbolic charity', inmates were occupied in processing wool; the regime took retribution on absconders, name callers and spoilers of work. Elsewhere circumstances varied. Knaresborough, although at one time consigning its refractory inmates to a 'black hole', also offered an agreeable raisin wine to conformists. But the general trend was harsh and repressive. Occasionally paupers were driven to rebellion, as at Roberttown in the Spen Valley when in 1760 the master had to be replaced. Individual actions were put down severely. At Heckmondwike in the same year Joseph Beecroft, having committed 'violent outrage', suffered a public whipping and three months detention, the last six weeks in solitary confinement.

Harsh tests were applied. Edward Peacock's pension was stopped at Arkengarthdale (Swaledale) in 1831 until he agreed to work on the roads. At Keld Joss Coates' widow had to sell her clock and other 'superfluous furniture' if she could not make do on her allowance.

The expenses of outdoor relief resulted in the Poor Law Amendment Act (1834) which aimed at cost-effective uniformity and central control from London. Workhouses were grouped into unions, and only paupers with no alternative sought refuge. 'If you are destitute, enter; if you refuse you cannot be destitute.' Thus ran the circular logic of the workhouse test. Outdoor relief was abolished. Families were split up. The commissioners were uncompromising: 'The separation must be entire and absolute between the sexes, who are to live, sleep and take their meals in totally distinct and separate parts of the building with an enclosed yard for each'.

In the quest for economy, regulation and penalties – 'catechisms of hell' – multiplied, incensing the whole nation. At a meeting in Bradford the commissioner for Yorkshire, Alfred Power, was rough-handled by a mob and beaten. In Huddersfield, a riotous crowd closed meetings of the Poor Law guardians. In several towns – Bradford, Dewsbury, Keighley – troops were drafted in to protect the authorities. At Haworth even the Revd Patrick Brontë fulminated, 'We will not submit to their bastilles. We will not live on their watery gruel and on their two ounces of cheese, and their fourteen ounces of bread daily.'

Yet much was won by sympathetic masters, as at Reeth (NR) where doles were given to families in serious need. Some Skipton children even enjoyed the occasional excursion to Morecambe.

The 'Hungry Forties' had a particular resonance in Hallamshire, where Ebenezer Elliott gained the reputation as 'the Masborough Corn Law Rhymer'. Chartist, moral crusader and satirist, Ebenezer campaigned against the so-called 'bread tax' in such lines as:

Dear sugar, dear tea and dear corn
Conspired with dear representation
To laugh worth and honour to scorn
And beggar the whole British nation.

His biting exposure of the deprivations of the poor helped to mobilise public opinion – which resulted in the abolition of the Corn Laws in 1846, and the opening of the ports to cheap foreign corn.

For the rest of the century workhouse conditions remained exacting. Able-bodied paupers were required to work at tasks like oakum-picking and stone breaking – parts of the punishment schedule in Her Majesty's prisons. Some houses, like Beverley's, had stone-breaking cells where fixed quantities of broken-up material had to be pushed through a grill. At the Easingwold Union Workhouse, tramps were discouraged from casual stays by offers of poorer food, as well as stone breaking. At Stokesley vagrants slept on bare boards until 1871.

The ultimate humiliation was the prospect of a pauper's funeral. After the parish coffin had conveyed the enshrouded corpse to the graveside, it was returned to the back of the church. A few coffins have survived – one is lodged in the Saltmarshe Chantry of Howden Minster; another is in Easingwold parish church.

Workhouse Farm cell, Holme on Spalding Moor.

Pauper's coffin, Howden Minster.

Traditional atonements

We may like to reflect that notions of punishment (and sometime atonement) are clear in certain festivals and customs:

1. Plough Stots

Over many parts of Yorkshire, up to the late nineteenth century, oddly attired young men carried a decorated plough around their village on Plough Monday, the first after Epiphany. In some areas they performed a version of a traditional mummers' play, starring St George, Beelzebub, Bosom Bet, Blether Dick *et al* engaged in slapstick sword combat. Householders who refused to give the stots (farm lads) a few coppers might well find a retributive diagonal furrow had been turned over their lawn.

2. Penny Hedge

About the year 1159 a wounded bear found shelter in the chapel of a hermit of Eskdaleside, but there it died. Its hunters, Lord Ugglebarney and friends, angered, beat the hermit but soon regretted their folly, recognising the penalty for killing a holy man was death. Forgiveness might be granted if they would conduct a yearly penance. So the hunters, and generations of their successors, cut wood with a penny knife and on Whitby harbour edge, on a receding tide, built a fence of ten uprights, interwoven with ten hazel strands, the two supports at each end being strong enough to withstand three tides. On Ascension Eve an Eskdaleside man cries, 'Out on ye! Out on ye!' and blows three blasts on a cow horn in expiation of this ancient crime.

3. The Burning of Bartle

Over 400 years ago Bartle, a reputed sheep stealer or horse thief, was tried at the court of West Witton (NR) and then burnt at the stake. His effigy is burnt on the Saturday night nearest to 24 August, St Bartholomew's Day, after a parade through the village.

4. The Lyke Wake Dirge

This is an ancient account of a dead soul making a purgatory journey barefoot over moorland covered with thorns and furze. May all our sins be forgiven as judgement is intoned!

Penny Hedge. (courtesy of the *Whitby Gazette*)

Bartle's end: mosaic by children of West Witton.

This yah neet, this yah neet
Ivery neet an' all,
Fire an' fleert, an' cannle leet
An' Chruist tak up thi saul.
When thoo frae hence has passed awee
Ivery neet an' all,
Ti Whinney Moor thoo comes at last
An' Christ tak up thi saul.

Those who completed the forty-two miles of the Lyke Wake Walk from Osmotherly to Ravenscar qualified for membership of the club and were entitled to wear its badge – a coffin!

Resolution

Yorkshire has never been short of resolute men, magnificently so in the case of t'awd squire, Sir Tatton Sykes (1772-1863), 4th baronet of Sledmere, who was very strict with his children. He once thrashed his son for bringing home from Harrow School a toothbrush – a clear sign of cissy conduct! Sir Tatton was also a superb horseman and a redoubtable pugilist who once routed two drovers who had mocked his squeaky voice and drunk his ale in a Pickering pub. When aged eighty, he ejected an uncooperative smoker from a Doncaster theatre box.

But resolution, tempered by rashness, is a different matter. The Railway King, George Hudson, self-made entrepreneur, having succeeded in bringing the railways to York, over-reached himself financially, transferring £40,000 from the York & North Midland into the Malton & Driffield Junction Railway without his directors' authorisation. 'His Steam Majesty' was exposed in the national papers, forced into bankruptcy and fled in shame to France. The sanctions of society can be very cruel against the mighty fallen.

Hudson off the rails. (courtesy of *Punch* Ltd).

chapter four

Corporal Punishment

In centuries past punishments were geared to retribution. Justice was rough, seen to be done, and often meted out in public view.

Ubiquitous duos

Stocks and pillory together were a feature of market places like Helmsley, Howden and Bridlington. Well into the nineteenth century, Leeds had stocks and pillory conveniently near the Moot Hall in Briggate. A variation was stocks and whipping post placed together, as happened outside Bolderstone church. Some communities equipped themselves with a considerable punitive armoury: Easingwold, for example, had a whipping post on the south side of the market place and a ducking stool on the north side, with stocks also available. Sometimes it was advantageous to punish several wrongdoers together – all of which must have made for a considerable public spectacle and entertainment.

Stocks

There is Biblical provenance for their use, assuming that meanings have not changed significantly in translation down the centuries. Thus we read in Job 13:27: 'Thou puttest my feet also in the stocks'. And 600 years BC it was reported: 'Then Pashur smote Jeremiah the prophet and put him in the stocks that were in the high gate of Benjamin' (Jeremiah 20:2).

Anglo-Saxon England adapted the idea further. A 'stoc' was an upper length of wood that could be moved up and down to accommodate the legs. In 1351 the Statute of Labourers recommended this sanction for workmen unwilling to accept wages at levels operating before the Black Death (1349). One effect of this catastrophic plague had been to make labour scarcer and more expensive.

In 1405 the provision of a set of stocks became compulsory in every town and village throughout the land, and for a wide variety of offences. The village constable was empowered to place in the stocks persons convicted of blasphemy, drinking, causing affray, breaking the Sabbath, Sunday gambling, refusing to help with the harvest, and much more. Many villages (e.g. Kirklington, near Ripon, in 1609) were fined for not properly maintaining their stocks. In practice these were often sited near the church, where churchwardens could keep an eye on the malefactor, or readjust the paper hat or notice proclaiming the crime. During the nineteenth century, churchwardens' evidence frequently resulted in a stocks sentence and these parish officers were required to assist the constable in physically compelling the convicted person to submit.

A surprising number of offences concerned drink or the breaking of the Sabbath (ie not attending church), or both. At Skipton the uniformed beadle armed with his trident staff of office, and accompanied by the parish wardens, toured the town during divine service, arresting drinkers encountered and escorting them to the stocks. It was rumoured that the investigators themselves found this spiritual exercise thirsty work! At times there must have been something of a queue for the stocks. During a churchwardens' tour of a Sheffield parish on a bright February Sunday morning in 1790, nine men were arrested for illicit tippling.

At Beverley the last man thought to have been set in the stocks by the market cross was Jim Brigham, drunk on a Sunday in 1853. The paper hat stating his offence was torn up a bystander, whilst a friend consoled him during his two-hour stint with a thoughtfully lit pipe. As late as 1860 John Gambles suffered in the Stanningley stocks from 2-8 p.m. for Sunday gambling. He was probably the butt, too, for witticisms on his name.

Barnsley's stocks on Market Hill were replaced (again) in 1844. In the same year a report in the *Pogmoor Almanac Register* commented: 'Two persons were placed in the stocks for two hours and were grinned at by a host of roguish lads and were a laughing stock for a numberless throng of upgrown citizens. Such an exhibition has not been witnessed in the town for more than twenty years'.

A sentence in Barnsley was generally served in two phases – the first facing uphill, the second downhill, with no support for the back. No wonder that those committed felt numb on release. Some had to be helped to walk.

In some instances the stocks might have been an effective social sanction. The offender, quite apart from being placed in an uncomfortable position for a long period, was at the mercy of the public who came to mock, humiliate and rejoice in 'cobblin'' the offender by throwing rotten eggs, offal, slaughter-house ordure, blood and rubbish of every kind – and at point blank range.

Stocks and pillory, Bridlington Old Town.

Stocks in Holy Trinity churchyard, Micklegate, York.

Unfortunately the situation could endanger public order. During the Sheffield corn riots in 1674 shops were smashed and delinquents rescued from the stocks, while the slender forces of the law were overwhelmed. In 1850 there was disorder at a Stokesley 'stocking' which marked the end of that punishment locally. Recurrent disorder may help to explain the frequent repairs to stocks, as noted in so many constables' and churchwardens' accounts.

The village stocks at Sutton-in-Craven, repaired in 1850, were little used thereafter, finding a new purpose as gateposts. Ecclesfield's disappeared overnight during the 1850s.

Although stocks were abolished in 1872, Yorkshire has many interesting survivals. Those at Settle were removed to the court house for use at local festivals. (One occasional incumbent, Tal Bradley, a fruit hawker, had, with help, managed to continue selling his oranges while immobilised). The Ripon stocks, last used in 1859 for Henry Lee and James Umpelby, who were found drunk and disorderly in Allhallowgate, remained in the marketplace until 1975 and are now in the courtyard of the Prison and Police Museum. At the approach to Holy Trinity church, Micklegate, York is a five-holed set... did they once accommodate one-legged miscreants?

Some stocks are located still on village greens, as at Aldborough and Bainbridge; others by market crosses – picturesquely at Ripley. A number are within church buildings (St Mary's, Beverley and Shiptonthorpe); and one a least is in a school – Driffield Secondary. At Bramley, Holbeck and Pool in Wharfedale, for example, the name lingers on in Stocks Hill.

Pillory, Ripon Prison and Police Museum.

'Necktrap'

Dubbed variously 'the necktrap' or 'shadow of the crucifixion', the pillory held the victim's head and hands in a wooden frame while the body remained standing. Like the stocks, it was already in use in Saxon times, often at crossroads, at the instigation of the lord of the manor. Henry III authorised its extended use in 1256. It punished offences like cheating, forgery, perjury, sedition, immorality, brawling and, during the seventeenth century, the printing of unlicensed books at York.

In 1420 Agnes, wife of John Piese, shipman of Hedon, was pilloried on Market Hill for selling two penny wheat loaves which were 'not useable and fusty'. Frequently punishments add comment to the social context. Thus, Hull ordinances of 1556 threatened to pillory anyone removing bricks or stones from the town walls – implying that the walls wanted repair. Some wrongdoers continued undeterred. James Ollerton of Bowling, a persistent 'barracter' or disturber of the peace, was ordered by the Leeds Sessions magistrates in 1677 to stand during market hours in the pillories of Leeds, Bradford and Halifax. Another triple pillory offender was George Metcalf of Askrigg, who, found guilty of forging a settlement pass, was obliged to stand on successive market days in the pillories of Bedale, Richmond and Middleham with the forged document attached to his hat.

In view of the Jacobite rebellion, the year 1715 was a dangerous time openly to be drinking the health of the Stuart Pretender, 'James III'. To do so in a Hull alehouse was to invite confrontation with the law on a charge of sedition. James Dobby's comeuppance took the form of a fine of £20, a prison remand – and the pillory.

Whatever the political temperature or the state of the nation, persecution of the oldest profession was continuous. At Leeds Quarter Sessions in 1754 Eleanor Hall (alias Nell Duxburry) was required to stand in the pillory for keeping a disorderly and infamous house. In 1808 two East Riding farm labourers, John Paul and Robert Eskritt, had spent time in the pillory on three

An offender in the pillory.

Old courthouse and stocks, Aldborough.

successive market days in Driffield for falsely accusing a local farmer of homosexual acts against them. Had the charge succeeded their employer might have been hanged. Some accusations were highly dubious. In September 1653, on the evidence of a Beverley man claiming to have seen her in the likeness of a cat and a bee, Elizabeth Roberts had been convicted of witchcraft and pilloried in Beverley, York and Bridlington.

The Driffield pillory was movable, but was generally kept in the market place. In 1810 a couple was arraigned there for fortune telling, which at that time still smacked of witchcraft.

Like the stocks, the pillory provided opportunities for rendering offenders 'publicly infamous' by heaping on them not only filth, ridicule and outrage, but violence and injury. 'Cobblin' 'em' was one thing; brickbats and even blinding were another. In 1815 the pillory was abandoned except for perjury, and altogether abolished in 1837, at the very outset of the Victorian era.

'Till the body shall be bloody'

From medieval times whipping was used in conjunction with pillory and stocks. Among the offences meriting the lash were vagrancy, hedge breaking, theft (especially sheep stealing), embezzlement, drunkenness, fortune telling and infringements of the local Assize of Bread and Ale (ie giving short or defective measure).

Further to an Act of 1530, vagrants were tied, largely naked, to a cart and flogged through the town 'till the body shall be bloody'. In Skipton the beadle whipped rogues and vagabonds out of town from the market cross. Sheep stealers were tied to a cart and flogged the length of the High Street. Vagrants, after due public whipping, were placed on oath to return to their native place, or to where they had lived for the past three years. From 1597 the law was modified so that offenders, including women, were naked only from the waist upwards. Local feelings no doubt allowed modest cover in the shadow of, say, Ripon Cathedral or York Minster.

In 1601 Alice Wright, deemed likely to become a charge on the poor rates of Kildwick in Craven, was whipped there and returned to Bolton Percy, her birthplace. For stealing a hat valued at 10d, Agnes Egglesfield was whipped and set in the stocks at Malton in 1605. Some years later a young servant girl, Jane Phillip, was publicly whipped in Stokesley market for stealing from her mistress at Nunthorpe Hall.

The Ecclesfield constable, in his accounts for 1642, showed some of the administrative extras involved in a judicial whipping. Two men had to be paid 3s for guarding Ellen Shaw prior to her appearance before Sir Francis Wortley; the constable's own charge for apprehending and accompanying her (1s 4d); paying Ronald Allen for going to Wakefield with her (3s); laying out 'vittuals' for her (1s 6d); paying a woman for the whipping (4d); and buying 'beare' for her afterwards. No wonder the escalating costs of crime were a subject of critical parochial debate in the middle of the seventeenth century.

Our forebears evidently believed that severe chastisement was fitting even for small transgressions. In 1761 Mary Hardman (alias Moll Fagg), convicted at Ardsley Quarter Sessions for the theft of a candlestick from the Red Bear Inn, was publicly whipped. Her alias suggests a degree of duplicity on previous convictions. At Ripon in 1778 Charles Dawson, too, appeared to be more than adequately punished for a poultry theft, consigned as he was to the house of correction for one month, and on three market days was whipped along the highway by the common crier. Due ceremony was upheld when Lydia Longbottom, formerly of Bingley, was whipped through the Wakefield thoroughfares for selling 'false and short yarn', the town bailiff, heading the procession, flourishing aloft the defective reel.

Comparing roughly similar crimes, but very different punishments, 100 years apart may be facile and inconclusive – but the temptation is strong! Both concerned rope thefts in Hull.

In 1819 William Randerson was flogged from Whitefriargate to Dock Bridge and back for the theft of 4st of old rope, followed by three months imprisonment. Almost exactly a century later a man called Kitching was merely placed on probation for two years for stealing a quantity of rope from the Albert Dock.

Well into the nineteenth century malefactors in Huddersfield were tied behind a cart and whipped from the Cloth Hall to the Dog Inn in Old Street... as our grandparents' grandparents might just have recalled! In many places the whipping post had been preferred, often standing by the market cross, or even attached to it, as at Richmond. Sets of irons secured the hands and feet. The savagery of such a beating, with leather thongs repeatedly tearing the shoulders, must have concentrated powerfully the minds of everyone present at these social occasions.

From 1791 the whipping of female vagrants ceased, and from 1820 the public flogging of women was abolished altogether. Forty years on men received the same concession. The flogging of a Wakefield man in June 1814 for poultry thefts was amongst the last recorded. Meantime, the birching of young criminals had begun in 1847. On 7 April 1937 nine boys aged between nine and thirteen appeared before the Doncaster West Riding Court charged with stealing fruit, nuts and sweets from a blind man selling them to cinemagoers. Eight were given three strokes, but the ninth was deemed medically unfit. Abolition had to await the Criminal Justice Act of 1948, except for prison mutineers or assaults on prison staff. Those, too, disappeared in 1967. The last flogging at Armley (Leeds) Gaol took place in 1926. Corporal punishment lingered on in state schools until 1986.

Locally the whipping post acquired a different kind of reputation as a 'kissing post' or 'bully block'. Groups of youths, noting a stranger, invited him to kiss the post and pay a fee – or be bumped against it.

Birching frame, Hull. (courtesy of Humberside Police)

Whipping post, Ripon.

Cucking and ducking

Although the cucking and ducking stool eventually became interchangeable terms in Yorkshire, there was once a real difference. The cucking stool, in its original sense, did not necessarily imply water, but rather a prolonged and uncomfortable exposure for the offender, fastened into a chair in front of his home, or loaded onto a tumbril and exhibited about the town, to be pelted by the mob. Ducking, however, meant just that – plunged under water. Secured to a seat at the end of a plank, the mischief maker was swung over and down – into pond, river or mere, generally three times.

In its Saxon context, 'cucking' (or 'gucking') meant scolding or brawling; but by Tudor times it had come to involve water, and the punitive plunge. The dramatists Beaumont and Fletcher, in *Tamer Tamed*, wrote:

> We'll ship them out in cuck stoles;
> Then they'll sail
> As brave Columbus did.

During Henry VIII's reign, Yorkshire wool spinners and carders accused of fraudulent work were apt to be set in the 'cukkyng-stole' and ducked. Up to the sixteenth century there was a good deal of 'carting about' the streets on hurdles for offences against the local Assizes of Bread and Ale – with the faulty loaf or flagon of bitter wine slung around the vendor's neck. In 1686 a Beverley sweet-shop owner, Martha Ferret, was ducked in the town pond off the York road for abusing and overcharging her customers. Another predictable category was fallen women. In 1620 Hull aldermen ruled that women 'faltie for bastards' should be carted about the town and ducked. In 1731 a new stool had to be installed at the South End, just east of the Humber/Hull confluence, 'for the benefit of scolds and unquiet women'.

At Ilkley seventeenth-century scolds were initially fined 6s 8d; failure to pay resulted in a ducking in the River Wharfe. At Elland Bridge 'alewives' were ducked in the Calder – 'alewife' being a general term for any noisy woman. At Scarborough the stool was located by the old pier where offenders were dipped in the German Ocean – the last being a Mrs Gamble in 1795.

On occasion the punishment went too far. At Bedale in 1776 a mob ducked Moll Cass, a renowned witch, nine times in the mill dam, from which she almost perished – but survived into her nineties.

Men, too, paid the penalty. Found guilty of lewd behaviour by Leeds Quarter Sessions in July 1694, Philip Saul was ducked on several consecutive days. The same sessions convicted his wife of like behaviour, causing neighbourly annoyance. From 1686 not only scolds but brewers of bad ale experienced the chilly waters beneath Stirk Bridge at Sowerby Bridge. Some offences were deemed so heinous that further punishment in pillory or stocks was salutary, and forgiveness publicly sought. We can but wonder that after all this humiliation and exposure the culprit could find sufficient breath for such atonement.

Earlier centuries, like our own, were often keen to will the means to restrain anti-social behaviour. At Helmsley Quarter Sessions in 1606 a complaint was registered that Langthorne had neither stocks nor 'cockinstole' for punishing miscreants. Alas for the deterrent theory, the same names recurred. Thus, in the North Riding records of 1609 Anne, wife of John Sweetinge of Middleton, Whernhowe, a notorious scold and a common drunkard given to lewd ways, was to be ducked whenever she offended.

As with other forms of public retribution the ducking stool gradually fell out of use. Skipton's, like many more, lasted until about 1770. Another conditioning factor, probably, was the cost of maintenance – even vandalism. Towards the end of the century Aberford's ratepayers had to find

Ducking chair. (courtesy of Rotunda Museum, Scarborough)

18s for a replacement. Values were changing and old ideas challenged. Of the few reminders, one is Ducking Stool Hill on Easingwold market place.

Branding

Branding had a long ancestry before it was institutionalised in Tudor times. In particular it was a way of literally marking out incorrigible vagrants. Under the vagrancy Act of 1547 idle but able-bodied persons could be judged by two JPs and branded on the shoulder with a bold V, made over as virtual slaves to an employer, and caused to work by beating, chaining or otherwise as deemed necessary. Any such slaves escaping and being recaptured could be branded with an S on the cheek. A second escape was punishable by death. While the worst elements in this barbaric law soon disappeared, branding persisted – M for malefactor, for instance, on face or hand. Cheek branding for various felonies was known in seventeenth-century Skipton. Elsewhere, F and A on both cheeks signified 'False Accuser' – a sharp example of how seriously defamation was regarded.

At Richmond Quarter Sessions 1610, several men were branded R for rogue. Convicted of begging in Wakefield in 1638, Thomas Garland of Attercliffe was branded on the shoulder: in the same year, Henry Illingworth of Sheffield, accused of lamb stealing, pleaded benefit of clergy before Barnsley magistrates. According to this legal escape clause, originally intended to favour clergymen, anyone satisfactorily demonstrating the ability to read from Psalm 51 might be spared, or their sentence reduced (see chapter two). Illingworth was perhaps fortunate merely to be branded T for thief on his left hand.

A contemporary hand branding was that of John Bek, labourer, convicted at Pontefract General Sessions Court of stealing three quarters of salt. As he had no chattels (moveable possessions offered as compensation) the hand that stole had to suffer permanent scarring.

Far worse was the fate of James Nayler of Ardsley in 1656. Accused of imposture and blasphemy, he suffered the pillory, a whipping, his tongue was bored and his forehead branded B with a red-hot iron. Subsequent medical treatment was unable to prevent his death.

In 1701 a felon was burnt R for rogue at Skipton's tollbooth. And as late as 1776 in York William Fawcett, expiating larceny offences, suffered a burnt hand, followed by one year of hard labour in Wakefield's house of correction.

Joug

The joug (from *jugum*, Latin for yoke or burden) was an iron collar placed round the defaulter's neck and the chain attached to a building, post, tree, door or market cross. Usually the victim stood but sometimes was obliged to kneel. Offences including scolding, sedition, slander, drunkenness, but more often were related specifically to Church laws against blasphemy, noisy behaviour during divine service, adultery or Sabbath breaking.

Favoured more in Scotland than England, the joug was in use locally here. Bridlington Priory church has, probably, the last survival in Yorkshire, fastened to the wall of the south-west tower. In past centuries it would certainly have been used for the public discomfiture of moral backsliders. Its very presence served as a warning. The joug, followed by public penance on a subsequent Sunday, may symbolise for us the hold that the church once had on the lives of parishioners.

The former joug in Wakefield Cathedral is now reduced to a few chain links on a wall at the base of the tower. An excellent replica is to be found in the small courtyard of the Ripon Prison and Police Museum.

Joug, Bridlington Priory church.

Scold's bridle

Like the joug, the bridle had proved its worth on the continent before its introduction here. Its basic design consisted of metal hoops brought down over the head, with a spiked plate positioned over the tongue so that the slightest movement brought the victim pain. She was thus led through the town, sometimes via the pillory, stocks, whipping post or ducking stool.

The bridle (or brank) was directed against false gossip, domestic chiding, street brawling and idle talk. In 1680 Cecily Eddon of Sinnington (NR) was bridled for eavesdropping under neighbours' windows. Hard as it may be to imagine inelegant scenes in Beverley, the Priests' Room in St Mary's church contains a pair of bridles alongside eighteenth-century stocks and pillory. A similar bridle is displayed in the Rotunda Museum, Scarborough.

Mutilation

For some prisoners, torture and mutilation were once facts of life – and death. Mutilation of the ears, threatened by Henry VIII as a punishment for vagrants, resurfaced in Halifax during the 1640s – seen, possibly, as a lesser penalty than the gibbet (see chapter six). According to the seventeenth-century antiquarian Brearcliffe, a Heptonstall man was 'nayled' on 1 February 1649, probably for theft. The poor man's ear was pinned to the stocks, pillory or gallows, and to add to the crowd's intrigue, he may have been given a tool (scissors, pliers) to try to free himself.

The phasing out of all forms of corporal punishment is now held to be a hallmark of a civilised society. It is interesting to reflect that the beating of schoolchildren was the last vestige, though whether parents should be allowed to apply 'moderate and reasonable' slaps is the subject of continuing debate. The cat o'nine tails, used in prisons as well as the Army and Navy, brings us neatly to our next range of punishments.

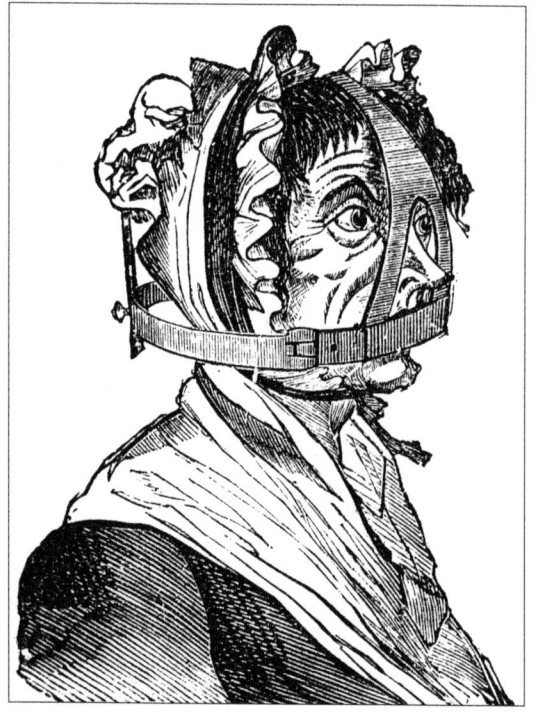

Scold bridled.

Bridle, St Mary's church, Beverley.

Beverley Minster misericord: a scold pulling her husband's hair.

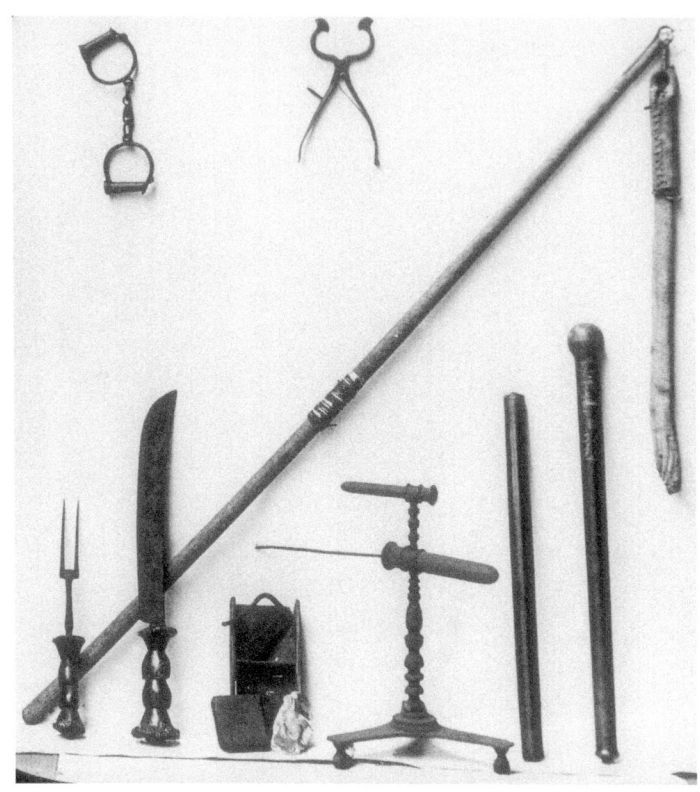

Left: Torture instruments. Note sugarloaf tongs and flail (diagonal) with knotted leather strips. (courtesy of Yorkshire Archaeological Society)

Below: Cat o' nine tails. (courtesy of Courthouse Museum, Ripon)

chapter five

Prisons and Transportation

Makeshift arrangements

From feudal times the lord of the manor was responsible for the incarceration of local prisoners whose crimes merited detention. During the sixteenth century, Thorne Castle and Sandal Castle were used for this purpose. Danby Castle in the Esk Valley has a dungeon at the base of a flight of steps, and Skipton Castle has two dungeons where prisoners were lodged prior to trial at York Castle.

At Knaresborough the vaulted base of the King's Tower (where Richard II made an overnight stay in 1399) often held a crowd of inmates. Holes remain where, reputedly, iron hoops once chained prisoners awaiting their turn to move nearer the flight of steps leading them to execution – a kind of 'death row'.

The dungeon at Bolton Castle was no more than a hole carved in solid rock at the base of a turret. Victims were dropped through a trap in the vaulting onto an earth floor. An arm bone was once found still manacled to the wall.

During the Civil War many Yorkshire castles were besieged or used as prisons. From May to August 1645 Parliamentary leader Sir John Meldrum confined Sir Hugh Cholmley's royalist supporters in Scarborough castle. Two years earlier Cholmley had miscalculatedly changed sides. After the war Oliver Cromwell had most of the castles 'slighted', rendering them unfit for future occupation.

At Rotherham the famous Chantry Chapel on the Bridge, set up for the use of religious travellers, was diverted in 1779 to house prisoners in the crypt's two cells, under the supervision of the town's deputy constable, who lived above.

Cellars, dungeons and outhouses were pressed into use. The village constable might lock up an otherwise harmless drunk for a few hours. More serious offenders would have to appear in court with the constable providing escort.

A number of communities had lock-ups associated with market toll-booths: at Bedale, close to the market cross; Guisborough and Settle had dungeons inside the former tollbooths. Until 1858 Skipton Old Town Hall's cellars accommodated casual prisoners, while the upper room was used as a court. The old Wetherby Town Hall, pulled down in 1845, had a lock-up and adjacent stocks. The fine Pontefract Town Hall, built in 1785, also provided court and lock-up facilities. At Hedon the old jail in the 1692 Town Hall has been transformed into the town clerk's office.

Some *ad hoc* arrangements must have been barely satisfactory, like the cellars of the White Swan at Wibsey, with a courtroom above, or the cell that became the snug at the Old Malt Shovel Inn at Harden, near Bingley. At least the Old Towzer, a small windowless stone lock-up, with constable's office (from around 1595) at the top of the steps near Holmfirth church permitted no tobacco or stimulants. Inebriants, or their supporters, had to pay 1d for release from the Penny Cells outside Snaith church. Here, as elsewhere, the sobering-up process was assisted by windows with tight grills through which no restoratives could filter.

Hunmanby's two 'black holes', for separate sexes, were built especially for drunks and fighters at the Martinmas hirings and fairs (see chapter three). Another unusual pair was at Luddesden (WR), built into the base of the Old School House (1825) at the corner of Old Lane. 'MIDGLEY' is carved into the left stone lintel, and 'WARLEY' on the right. As the parish boundary once separated the two, it was thought administratively tidy to lock up miscreants in the appropriate place.

Sometimes, the better to supervise his charges, the constable received personal lodging attached. At Elland a square building (1821, demolished in 1963) facing the Town Hall had, apart from its cells, a dwelling either for the constable or other parish officials like the pinder, who impounded stray animals. A legend above the doorway read, 'Whoso keeps the law is wise'.

The Illingworth 'clink', dating from 1823, was still in occasional use at the end of the nineteenth century. The bolt-studded door was reinforced by an iron sheet to repel violent sympathisers. Occasionally the constable had to provide beds for all four cells, and to escort serious offenders the next day to court at Halifax. One wonders how effective the moral text on a stone tablet over the door was:

> Let him that steals go steal no more
> But rather let him labour, working with
> His hands the thing which is good, that
> He may have to give to him that needeth

More down to earth were the stocks, still in place, to the left.

Many lock-ups were vulnerable. At Thornton le Dale the 'black hole' used to lodge passing tramps and inebriates was successfully stormed in 1850 by a group of local men hoping to release a woman.

Chantry Chapel, Rotherham.

Penny cells, Snaith.

Illingworth Old Clink, with stocks, left.

Scarcely more hospitable would have been the 'den' opening onto the Kirkgate pavement in Ripon, used by the borough police between 1838 and 1877. The erection of police stations in the 1840s brought purpose-built cells, supervised by a burgeoning professional force, making redundant the casual lock-ups. The Driffield police station on Eastgate North, now a private house, was designed by H.F. Lockwood in 1843 and had two cells, as well as a superintendent's accommodation – a substantial improvement on the old outhouse stable behind the Red Lion in Middle Street North! Not to be missed is the picturesque conical-topped house opposite the Staveley Arms at North Stainley (NR), while at Heptonstall (WR) the 'dungeon' is a cellar beneath the former Co-op.

Debtors' prisons

Up to the eighteenth century most prisoners were either debtors or awaiting trial. Many gaols opened for general prisoners eventually became debtors prisons, other felons having transferred elsewhere: thus, the former archbishop's court house at Ripon, having become the gaol for the Liberty, eventually took debtors only (see chapter one).

While sheriffs, JPs and other senior churchmen bore overall responsibility for prisons, day-to-day control was exercised by gaolers and their assistant turnkeys, unsalaried officials whose income derived directly from their prisoners and supporters. Generally uneducated men, they charged what their human traffic could bear – for admission, a cell with a window, freedom

North Stainley lock-up.

Midgley and Warley cells.

from shackles, beds, blankets, lights, fires and furniture. At Batley a better-off inmate paid 4d a night, a yeoman 2d, while two ordinary men could share a bed for 3d. Others made do with straw palliasses and rags.

Paradoxically, access to money brought privileges. Those without ate poorly and were confined to dirt, extortion, brutality and neglect: those backed by influential friends could buy refreshment and enjoy some degree of liberty, even living off the premises. At the Hanson Lane Prison, Halifax, bedtime was officially 9.30 p.m. but liquor could be brought in until 10 p.m. Drink was a problem leading to squalor, intimidation and violence. 'Chummage' was a protection racket by which new entrants sought to ingratiate themselves with turnkeys and chosen inmates. Money gained friends, day passes, entertainment, women, games, gambling – frequently compounding original arrears.

Medical aid was minimal. Lice and typhus (gaol fever) were common. Discharged prisoners took their untreated conditions back into the community. Venereal disease was a consequence of mixed prisons where promiscuity was rife. Opportunities for exercise were very limited, often non-existent. Education and moral instruction were nugatory. Prisoners with modest means were permitted to make simple garments, nets, garters, purses, laces to sell to visitors. Very occasionally craftsmen like joiners or cobblers were enabled to earn a little money.

Reports highly critical of Yorkshire prisons, which were no worse than elsewhere, were made by the penal reformer John Howard (1726-90), based on several visits he made between 1773 and 1788. Their very air was so foul, he asserted, that his clothes stank outside. Knaresborough's rat-infested gaol for town debtors received special condemnation. A common sewer ran through the main room, which had an earth floor and no fireplace. This institution, long demolished, has a cell door displayed in the Ripon Museum; noteworthy is the cylindrical hatch through which food was passed.

Leg irons. (courtesy of York Museums)

Howard called for more humane regimes, better accommodation, ventilation, sanitation, plain nutritious food, organised work, religious education and physical exercise. He specially lambasted the discriminatory charges. Gaolers needed to be replaced by trained salaried officers.

But most abuses continued. Better than most was the Debtors Prison at York, built between 1701 and 1705 by local architect William Wakefield, and now part of the Castle Museum.

Conditions were clean and dry, and some inmates were allowed to mingle with visitors in the small yard. Shielded by a glass cover is some instructive graffiti etched by Thomas Smith, aged twenty-eight, who was hanged in 1820 for sheep stealing: 'This prison is a house of care, a grave for man alive, a touchstone to try a friend, no place for a man to thrive'. In order to meet his Maker, Smith would have no great gauntlet to run, as since 1802 executions had taken place at the castle instead of the Knavesmire.

Unusually carefree, indeed, was the welcome at Rothwell, where during the first half of the nineteenth century conditions were quite good and the ethos surprisingly relaxed. Camaraderie was encouraged – there was even a satirical welcoming song, whose flavour is clear in the following verse:

> Welcome, welcome, brother debtor
> To this poor but merry place,
> Where no bailiff, bum or setter
> Dares to show his frightful face.

Much savoured were mock trials, practical jokes, quoits, skittles, diversions and entertainments. Permission to keep canaries was another humane touch.

YORK CASTLE.

Each Debtor to pay 6d. (in advance) every Saturday for the use of Chairs, Tables, Drawers, Looking-Glass, Fender, Fire-Irons, Frypan, and Candlestick, in the room they occupy.

GEO. HOWARD,
23, Davygate, YORK.

1st Jan., 1869.

York Castle costs, 1869. (courtesy of York Museums)

Debtors prison, York.

Left: Condemned cell, York.

Below: Seventeenth-century neck iron. (courtesy of Wakefield Museum)

> CITY of YORK. **To the Keeper of his Majesty's Gaol the House of Correction, in and for the City of York and County of the same City.**
>
> RECEIVE into your Custody the Body of Robert Bean herewith sent unto you, being charged before me, one of his Majesty's Justices of the Peace for the City of York and County of the same City, upon the Oath of Mary Tate Robert Watson and others on suspicion of feloniously stealing on Saturday last at the parish of Saint Sampson in the said one piece of pattent cord the property of James Shaw
>
> Keep him therefore in safe Custody, until discharged by due Course of Law. Given under my Hand and Seal this 4th Day of November in the Year of our Lord 1817.

Notice of new prisoner. (courtesy of York Museums)

An occasional inmate of the King Street Gaol in Sheffield was Joseph Mather, an impoverished but sharp critic of the penal system. When Col Althorpe, the volunteers' commander, ordered troops into a crowd in 1795, killing two and wounding others, Mather accused him of murderous repression: 'What the bloody tyrant meant/ Was murder without precedent'.

What this poet lacked in material things he made up for in fighting spirit. A vast crowd attended his funeral in 1804.

By the 1820s new ideas in criminal justice were being pursued by the home secretary, Sir Robert Peel. A Gaols Act in 1823 provided women warders for female prisoners. At Doncaster the building of the borough gaol – 'the fortress' – in 1829, accommodating both debtors and other felons, can be seen as a transitional institution. A further Act of 1835 introduced prison inspectors, and four years later general rules were to be applied in all prisons. From 1861 individuals could plead bankruptcy, thus keeping most debtors from custody.

Then in 1868 – a highly significant year – came the end of transportation, public executions and the abolition of debtors prisons. Henceforth, only fraud or refusal to pay merited imprisonment for debt.

Houses of correction

Their origin lay in a Tudor anti-vagrancy scheme of 1576 by which justices of the peace, through a local poor rate, were to provide shelter, work and training for the sturdy rogues, idlers, beggars and itinerants who were seen as a scourge of the Elizabethan countryside. Yorkshire's first house was probably at Wakefield in 1595, followed by Beverley and York (1611) and Richmond (1620), with others at Pickering, Thirsk and Whitby by 1636.

Their prime function was penal, and they came to accommodate all sorts and conditions of 'idle, lewd and disorderly persons', those awaiting trial, thieves, feckless families, and felons generally. During the 1650s Quakers were sent to Wakefield for refusing oaths of allegiance and militia service, whilst under the Clarendon Code (1661-64) Roman Catholic and nonconformist ministers were sometimes sent to houses of correction for refusing the Thirty-Nine Articles of the Church of England. By the end of the century many Yorkshire 'houses' were *de facto* prisons. Vagrants continued to be discouraged. In 1706 Mary Watson was whipped from Ripon, after detention, and returned to Kendal, her birthplace.

Diet was basic and work enforced. Pickering came to specialise in wool products, knitting and jerseys; Wakefield established a tradition of weaving and dressing wool, though from 1709 separate workrooms for men and women had to be arranged, owing to 'several lewdnesses having been committed'. Up to 1727 the 'maister' treated the inmates like debtors, charging them where possible for their keep, for unlocking their leg irons and for selling their work.

Staff in houses of correction were untrained and there were many cases of suspension, fines and removal from office. In 1764, two governors, Downes of Knaresborough and Waugh of Wakefield, were each fined £20 (a quarter of their salary) for allowing prisoners to escape.

Accordingly, discipline was harsh. Disorderly or recalcitrant prisoners were whipped. A routine was necessary to instil order, if not always respect. At Richmond in 1716 Margaret Anderson, 'a drunken idle Scottish woman who had cursed the King… is to be put to work and whipped if necessary'. Some prisoners were 'ironed' – chained to a wall to prevent escape, or for a cooling-off period.

From its foundation in 1783 a strict regime was implemented at Northallerton. Many of the Sheffield Chartists conspiring to breach the peace with guns, bombs, daggers etc were brought here from the York Spring Assizes in 1840.

In 1834 new measures were introduced, based upon experience deemed successful in America. Under the 'silent system', prisoners were forbidden to speak to one another, on pain of flogging. Men were reported more than women, yet one of the earliest inspectors, the Revd Whitworth Russell averred in 1835 that 'with women… I would have silence and segregation strictly observed, for women contaminate one another even more than men do'. Russell was not alone in thinking that female inmates caused difficulties disproportionate to their numbers.

The separate system brought solitary confinement. In some houses, including Wakefield, prisoners had to wear masks in the exercise yard so as not to be recognised. But separateness in workrooms was hard to enforce, and solitary confinement soon resulted in some nervous breakdowns. 'Separate and silent' required a high ratio of staff to prisoners, and during the 1860s these regimes were abandoned. More effective were short confinements in a 'black hole' on a restricted diet of bread and water, no heating and a plank bed.

The treadmill, invented in 1817 by William Cubitt, an Ipswich engineer, was universally hated. It consisted of a cylindrical drum, with a diameter of about 5ft and with twenty-four steps around the edge. Lines of prisoners, screened from one another, 'walked' uphill for twenty minutes at a time: men were compelled to take up to 12,000 steps a day, women up to 10,000 – the equivalent of walking up a considerable hillside.

Although as a rule its prime purpose was punishment, the treadmill was later harnessed to economic production. At Beverley it produced whiting from chalk quarried off the nearby Westwood. At Northallerton and Wakefield it was used for bone-crushing and grinding.

A contemporary folk song shows some interesting sequences:

At six o'clock our turnkey comes in
With a bunch of keys in his hand.
Come, come, my lads, step up and grind
And tread the wheel till breakfast time.

At eight o'clock our skilly comes in,
Sometimes thick and sometimes thin,
And if one word we chance to say
It's bread and water all day.

At nine o'clock the bell does ring
All on the trap, boys, we must swing.
Come pray, my lads, to be on time
The wheel to tread and the corn to grind.

At ten o'clock the doctor comes round
With a pen and paper in his hand,
And if we say we are not ill
It's all next day to the treading mill.

Treadmill, Hull. (courtesy HM Prison, Hull)

Many prisoners found the mill extremely enervating. It induced hot sweats, nausea and breathing troubles. As the last verse hints, many feigned illness in the hope of being excused.

As criticisms mounted in the 1860s there was a decline in the treadmill's use. During a church congress at York in 1877 several bishops took themselves off to the castle to experience the dreaded wheel for themselves. From that day the condemnation of the Church was assured, but formal abolition had to wait until 1898.

Meantime many 'houses' had turned to oakum picking. Old ropes were cut into lengths to be cleaned, shredded into strands, and the residual tar removed by swinging each strand across a hook, or the prisoner's knee. The completed oakum was sold for caulking the seams of ships' decks, for which there was an inexhaustible demand, hence 'money for old rope'. Occasionally oakum was diverted to making cheap mats or to fill prison mattresses. Thus oakum picking became part of mid-Victorian scheme of hard labour, tedious, unpleasant and dusty, resulting in sore, even bleeding hands.

With the Prisons Act (1877) the smaller houses of correction disappeared. Ten years later the old Ripon house was given a new lease under the West Riding Constabulary which replaced the Ripon Borough Police Force. Many of the old routines were absorbed into the new dispensation, but the trend was towards larger, almost regional prisons.

Nineteenth-century developments

Beverley's new 'house', set up in Norfolk Street in 1814, provided for 100 convicts, vagrants and 'misdemeants', including women. Short haircuts and uniform were obligatory. Stone breaking for road repair was a common task for men; and for both sexes the treadmill operated from 1823.

Old institutions like Wakefield continued to evolve. A change of governor often brought fresh ideas. Edward Shepherd, an unusually progressive and enlightened governor, held office from 1832 until 1864. Abolishing both flogging and the treadmill, he introduced basic education, and stepped up incentives for good work and behaviour in such trades as wool dressing, shoe and mat making. Good conduct was rewarded with better food – but for disruptive prisoners he alternated short periods in the dark cell on a bread and water diet with a normal diet. He introduced also a scheme for resettlement grants on prisoners' release.

Hardly had Shepherd retired, however, than a new Prison Act restored tighter regimes, reaffirming flogging and solitary confinement – and the treadmill, which at Wakefield now provided a power source for prison machinery.

The new jail, opened in 1867, continued to stress the work principle – adding carpentry, wheel making, agricultural tools and basketry in the hope, not always realised, that skills thus learned might have a transfer value back in civil life. The circular exercise yards round which prisoners marched, with subdued satirical singing, earned Wakefield the derisive nickname, the 'Mulberry Bush'.

At Ripon the new prison, built in 1816 and adjacent to the old house of correction, became the Liberty Gaol. Male offenders generally served short sentences for bastardy, family neglect, poaching, larceny, and drunk and disorderly behaviour. By the 1830s the diet included bread, meat, potatoes, soup and oatmeal gruel. A few female prisoners were occupied with domestic and cleaning tasks, and from 1837 the governor's wife acted as matron.

Hard labour included the treadmill and the crank – an iron box with a metal handle attached, erected on a solid base in certain cells, and standing at shoulder height. Prisoners were required to turn the handle up to 10,000 times a day, a dial plate recording the number of turns. With each revolution a circle of cups dipped into a base of sand and opened at the top. The crank was a deliberately tiring and pointless punishment, but the prisoner's meal depended on its completion. The origin of the label 'screw' for warder probably derives from the tightening of a screw on the crank to make the handle still harder to move.

A variation was shot drill: making prisoners, up to forty-five years of age, lift and carry for a few paces a cannon ball weighing about 32lb (15kg), or pass it along a line of inmates.

By the mid-century, houses of correction and prisons were becoming more regularised and comparable. A governmental decree of 1843, for example, attempted to bring all prison diets to a fair standard, as at Ripon. Cocoa was added to the list and in 1864 suet pudding was recommended. Overall, thereafter, prison diet changed little for the rest of the century.

'The Country Castle'

Built in 1847 as Leeds Borough Gaol, Armley maintained a tough physical regime throughout the Victorian period: 'hard bed, hard fare, hard labour,' ran a contemporary dictum. For the first month the prisoner rested on a bare plank; a mattress had to be earned by good behaviour. Thereafter, clean underclothes were issued once a week, and bed sheets once a month – privileges not universal, even for women. A tepid bath was allowed once a month. One letter could be sent and received. At exercise times, prisoners walked round and round, keeping a steady pace and without talking. A variety of manual work, including mat making, was supervised by taskmasters. Many cells were fitted with crank machines.

Except in circumstances of 'urgent necessity', chains, fetters and handcuffs to restrain had been banned in 1865, but in his report four years later the governor claimed that women, unrulier than the men, were likelier to be 'ironed' for short periods. It is surprising, perhaps, that some female

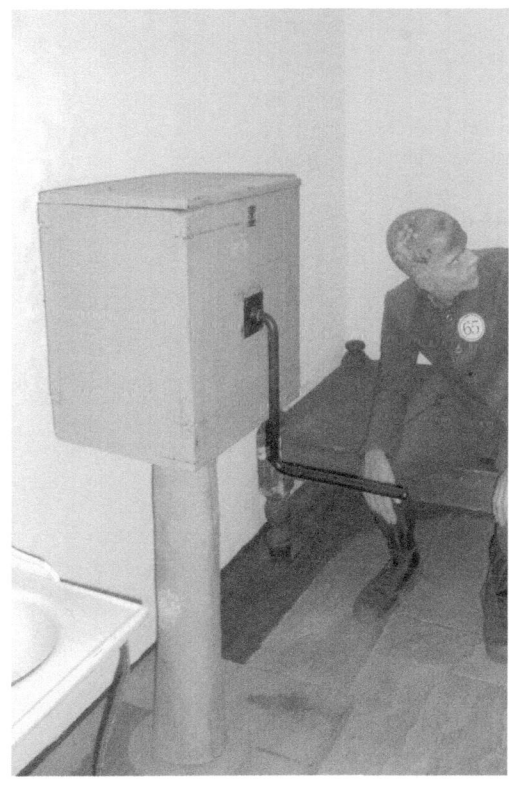

Crank. (courtesy of Ripon Prison and Police Museum)

cells at Armley had to be fitted with stocks! Bad language proved such an intractable problem in the women's ablutions that extra walls were built around them to confine bad talk. And women proved no less deserving of the 'dark cell' punishment – plank bed, no heating, no exercise, and bread and water diet. But at least they were spared flogging.

Hull

The first recorded prison was in the market place early in the fourteenth century. From 1829 the prison was the United Gaol and House of Correction, built in five radial blocks, and situated near the Albert Dock. It followed a general pattern of poor accommodation for ragged and neglected prisoners, subjection to the treadwheel and the silent system from the 1830s, and the crank from about 1850. The customary industrial jobs were available: mats, tailoring, shoes, and carpentry, with laundry and sewing for women. In 1848 inspectors recommended prison dress, and felt that uniform for officers might heighten all-round respect. By 1857 there was a Discharged Prisoners Aid Society.

Hull's main problem was overcrowding, always a threat to discipline – and reluctance on the part of the town council to provide new premises, despite adverse reports. In 1869 a new prison was built on Hedon Road, opening with 388 cells, plus eleven punishment cells. The routine was tough, especially in the first month. Cells, 10 ft by 7ft, had no luxuries – just a bare wooden bed with sheets and blankets, stool, water tin, bucket… Meals were taken in the cell. Much time was spent there, including work (chopping wood and unpacking materials for more experienced prisoners). Daily chapel and the exercise yard offered little human contact. During the first six months there were no visits and no letters. After that, one visitor and one letter per month could be received.

Subsequently the prisoner was allowed to mix with others, but talking was restricted. Work was extended to include stone breaking, foundry work, making fish boxes and mail bags, for which modest payments were made. Good behaviour earned mattresses. At the third stage letters and visits were allowed, and earnings increased. The fourth stage gave better food, including more meat and cocoa.

For some years both sexes suffered the treadmill, harnessed to produce whiting, and teasing oakum. Infringements of discipline reduced privileges. Flogging remained a further sanction for men.

Nationwide, governors and chaplains were agreed that much crime was caused by bad habits like fecklessness and drink, together with profound ignorance. It was estimated that about half of all prisoners could not repeat the Lord's Prayer, and one in ten had heard of neither their Saviour nor their Queen. Nearly one in five, mostly men, did not know the months of the year.

To the end of the century punishments could be severe. In August 1897, during the Bishop Wilton Show (ER), Sam Higgins and Charles Granvill, vagrants, stole from a house eight eggs valued at 4s, for which they received fourteen days hard labour in York Castle.

Reformatories and industrial schools

Riotous youth was ever a problem! A meeting of JPs at Knaresborough in 1787 admitted 'frequent and great disorders from fairs, feasts and rushbearings'. Parents were urged to keep children and young servants 'to their proper employment at home,' rather than be drawn into street disturbances, idleness and dissipation. Thanks were given to clergy, constables, churchwardens and principal inhabitants – a thin list indeed of the contemporary agencies working for law and order among the young.

The growing interest of Church and State in elementary education from the 1830s raised the question of how public institutions should cope with youngsters from backgrounds of deprivation, instability and criminality. From 1854, under the Youthful Offenders Act, under-sixteens could be hived off to reformatory schools for periods of two to five years, with an emphasis on hard physical labour which might prove redemptive. Hitherto, such youngsters had been sent to houses of correction, which often confirmed them in bad habits.

Problems of recruiting sympathetic but firm staff were illustrated by events at the Leeds Moral and Industrial School, which opened in 1848, surviving until 1902. Two reverend heads left, unable to cope with the challenges. Some children came in as boarders from workhouses, later to be fostered out. Although absconding was a regular problem, for many youngsters the school proved a haven. Many found success in industrial and domestic jobs.

The beginnings of the York Industrial Schools can be traced to the Wesley Place Sunday school, a mid-century ragged school attended by youngsters considered too poor and unkempt to qualify for other Sunday schools. The boys' school opened in Marygate in 1853 for children committed for larceny, burglary, arson and found uncontrollable at home. Some were sent from other Yorkshire towns. This school lasted until 1921. The girls' school, after an interregnum in Leeds, was re-established in Lowther Street in 1877, and concentrated on needlework, laundry, drill, cooking etc, with occasional diversions like Morris dancing. There was no corporal punishment, but privileges were restricted and offenders consigned to a distant lighted room. This institution survived until 1930.

Further to the various Church-backed initiatives, the Industrial Schools Act of 1857 allowed magistrates to commit for boarding juvenile beggars, those beyond control and those guilty of less serious offences. The same year saw the foundation of the Leeds Society for the reformation of juvenile offenders. Some forty children were admitted, learning skills in shoemaking, woodwork, farming and domestic work as well as reading and writing. Much emphasis was placed on trust and the young persons were given considerable freedom.

Similar establishments set up for boys were the Castle Howard Reformatory School and the Calder Farm Reformatory at Mirfield. The latter's aims were 'to restrain what is evil, and to encourage in what is good by admonition, rewards and punishments, adapted to their respective cases and characters'. Apart from farm work and the customary workshops, great attention was given to religious and moral education. Early boarding units for girls were the West Riding Reformatory, Doncaster and the Howard Hill School, Sheffield. The Ripon Industrial School for girls, established in 1862, took in some forty orphans aged seven to fourteen, preparing them mainly for domestic service.

Although 'reformatory' indicated a moral turning from crime and 'industrial' implied the teaching of skills, in practice these institutions were hardly distinguishable in their routines. The point is illustrated by the Industrial Schools Act of 1866 which took a preventive flavour, providing a basic social and industrial training for children at risk: orphans, 'refractory children' and those of clear criminal parentage.

Punishments – official ones, at least – showed little variation: they included cancellation of home leave; forfeiture of meals; less or poorer food; confinement in a lit room for up to three days with a diet of bread, gruel, milk and water; 'moderate personal correction', with up to twelve strokes of the birch according to age and offence (for boys only). Officially, girls were rarely submitted to corporal punishment. Some institutions drew up marks systems which earned small amounts of pocket money. Punishment books were available to the governing committee.

The Roman Catholic authorities showed commendable initiative. At Halifax the Shibden Industrial School set up in 1877 admitted up to the age of fourteen young offenders, orphans, truants and others thought to be in need. This school enjoyed a good reputation for self sufficiency, discipline and cleanliness. The children were taught the 3Rs and much religious and moral training. Emphasis was placed on work with useful potential – shoemaking, woodwork, printing, farming, baking, painting. But these youngsters were rarely allowed home.

More vicissitudes were suffered at the Yorkshire Catholic Reformatory School for Boys (later St William's School) near Market Weighton. Again, general and religious education was supported by practical work and experiments were made with promotions to prefect, corporal, sergeant – though disappointments were frequent. Criticisms were repeatedly made by inspectors against beatings, the dark cells, baths, food and recreational facilities.

In general there were problems with aftercare. To return to slum backgrounds was often to become reimmersed in deprivation and crime. Some young men found another kind of discipline in Army careers.

As probation took over after the Young Offenders Act (1907) industrial schools declined, but some reformatories lingered on, Shibden's until 1932. Others were adapted as approved schools. From 1902 the Borstal system provided an exacting physical routine for sixteen to twenty-three-year-olds who had already been in serious trouble. Set up at Borstal, Kent, the movement was influenced by the public-school tradition of house systems, physical education and games, physical chastisement and the moral influence of the staff. An intriguing experiment was the Juvenile Adult Reformatory established at Hull Prison in 1906. Not only was work given by a sympathetic ship owner, but education was supervised from an unlikely but effective source – Mr G.H. Gore, headmaster of Hymers College, Hull, whose more academic students came from privileged backgrounds.

As youth continued to be a problem, the idea of a 'short sharp shock' was revived with the detention centres under the Criminal Justice Act of 1948.

Banishment and transportation

Over many centuries expulsion from the realm was the fate of many a malefactor. Some jumped before they were pushed, like Drogo de Bevere, a Flemish adventurer who, having wed the niece of William the Conqueror, murdered her at Skipsea Castle before fleeing to France. It is rumoured that her White Lady stayed behind to haunt the precincts.

Piers Gaveston, favourite of Edward II, received the honour and castle of Knaresborough, but was banished in 1311 when the Yorkshire barons found his conceit insufferable. His mistake was to return when noble tempers cooled. Besieged in Scarborough Castle he surrendered, only to be beheaded at Warwick Castle.

At a lower social level, persistent poaching occasionally resulted in banishment. John Abbas of Rosedale was outlawed for hart shooting near Goathland in 1325, while Will of Filey was similarly removed for hare hunting in 1334 in the Royal Forest of Pickering.

In Elizabethan times while many recusant priests lost their livings, some suffered further sanctions. Sir Thomas Bowlton, a Catholic priest was imprisoned in York Castle in 1558, suffering a further eight years in the Hull blockhouse before final banishment.

The expedience of permanently disposing of unwelcome persons, short of execution, was raised to government principle in 1718 by an Act authorising transportation to 'His Majesty's Colonies or Plantations in America', particularly Virginia and Maryland. Seven years was the usual sentence. Any attempt to return earlier could result in hanging. Many offences qualified – thefts of money, goods, receiving or robbery with violence, rape, coining, forgery, embezzlement and, of course, sheep stealing and infringement of the Game Laws.

So it came to pass that in 1723 John Baker, who had stolen 9s from John Willson and broken out of Pontefact Gaol, was sentenced to seven years at York Assizes, the judge doubtless intoning the customary dismissal – 'It is therefore ordered and ajudged by this court that you be transported upon the seas, beyond the seas, to such a place as His Majesty shall think fit'. Not long in following was Joyce Birkenshaw, referred from Rotherham Quarter Sessions to York for petty larcenies.

Doubtless the presiding judge took into account the fact that Elizabeth Pickersgill of Ripon had already been convicted for the theft of two turkeys, but the purloining of one silver spoon in 1737 was enough for her to be sent to New England. Whether Dawn Richardson, spinster of Etton, near Beverley, was an inveterate miscreant is unknown, but in 1763 she received seven years for filching three iron screws.

Such examples can be multiplied endlessly. Judith Grant of Hull was sent away in 1745 for seven years for stealing two linen aprons; George Beecroft of Yarm stole 3lbs of butter, the property of John Whaley, in 1766; John Naylor, a Ripon maltster, stole coal and apparently welcomed transportation in 1836 to Van Dieman's Land as a means of escaping from his wife!

The task of shipping abroad vast numbers of convicts was delegated to government contractors, often merchants experienced in colonial conditions. When the war with America began in 1776, prisoners were held in hulks in the River Thames, but soon Australia was the destination – Botany Bay, Norfolk Island and Van Dieman's Land (Tasmania). Every woman transported earned the contractor £8, £10 for an unskilled man, and £15 for an approved craftsman. Put aboard ship in Hull or London, the convicts were shackled below decks in overcrowded and insanitary conditions, with poor food and little medical attention. Seasickness and lack of ventilation added to their distress.

Few informed persons would have accepted Lord Ellenborough's view, expressed at the turn of the century, that transportation was no more than 'a summer airing by an easy migration to a milder climate'. Unpleasant times lay ahead. Many men were directed to road building into the mountains of New South Wales, clearing ditches, building, or from 1822 the construction of Macquarrie Harbour. A military guard precluded any chance of escape. Officers had the pick of female servants. Many women were sent to Parramatta, near Sydney, to labour in woollen factories.

While many convicts never made the return journey to Yorkshire, one extraordinary Pateley Bridge man did so twice. Involved in the murder of a constable and the savage beating of a gamekeeper, Elisha Sinclair (or Sinkler) served his time in Australia before returning to his old pursuits of violent affrays. Convicted for stabbing, he was again transported, this time for life. Oddly he helped to quell a riot in 1856, obtaining the Queen's pardon and returning to his homeland once more to continue his brushes with the law.

A remarkable villainous family man, and leader of an opportunist gang, was Snowden Dunhill of Spaldington (ER). Convicted in 1813 of a series of farm burglaries he spent six years aboard a Thames hulk, but was discharged early for good behaviour. Meantime, his wife Sarah had been transported for picking pockets at Hull Fair, a son, William, was transported for fourteen years but died on arrival, and another son, George, a Beverley labourer, was convicted of the theft of a bushel of wheat and transported, as was a stepson, Robert Taylor. Transported again for various thefts, Snowden managed to write his life story, eventually printed by William Pratt of Howden. In 1833 he obtained his freedom and was reunited with his wife and daughter in Hobart. Although he was starting to regret his past life, his troubles with the law continued. His book helped to perpetuate his memory and freebooter reputation. It is a revealing document of weakness and folly, conveying a first-hand view of criminal motivation – and the doubtful deterrent value even of transportation.

Other cases, in retrospect, seem pathetic. The Wakefield Quarter Sessions recommended John Carless to life transportation in 1842 for burglariously entering Mirfield Parish church. The following year two young Howden men stole a box of ribbons and somewhat insensitively tried to sell them to the wife of the Yokefleet constable, thus earning seven years hard graft on the developing roads of the Australian outback.

Colonial politics, expense, penal reform, a more humane spirit – these were some of the factors underlying the abolition of transportation in 1850. By the last quarter of the century, prison with hard labour (penal servitude) was the last serious sanction, apart from the death penalty, for treasonable offences and murder.

Press gang

Since medieval times military service had been used as a punishment (depending on a judge's discretion), but the activities of a press gang in Georgian times amounted to the kidnapping and forcible detention in HM Royal Navy of any able-bodied man in the seventeen to fifty-five age group. Although coastal towns were most vulnerable, in 1777 the press gang reached York in a pinnace and several yawls in order to bring back recruits to Hull. Even in the West Riding there was anxiety. On 6 August 1779 – harvest season – Richard Mawood, deputy clerk of the peace, Tadcaster, acting on behalf of His Majesty's JP Special Sessions, issued an immunity to itinerant labourers that they should not be 'liable to be pressed or in any way molested' in the furtherance of their employment.

Nor were other seafarers immune from capture. Whaling captains returning from Arctic waters frequently allowed young crew members to disembark on quiet coastal stretches rather than risk being arrested in the streets or alehouses of Hull and Whitby. In 1792 a group of Whitby seamen, challenged by the gang, savagely routed them and destroyed their rendezvous in Haggersgate. But the Spring Assizes, York 1793 resulted in riot leaders William Atkinson (eighty) being hanged, and Hannah Hobson transported. In *Sylvia's Lovers,* Elizabeth Gaskell presented another version of this affray at 'Monkshaven'.

Five years later came the Blenheim incident in Hull. After a chase up the Humber the whaler *Blenheim* was boarded by a naval party – which was fought off by a determined crew wielding spikes, spears and flensing knives. Two ratings were killed and there were many injuries. Captain Mitchinson of the Blenheim may, or may not, have been locked out of danger by his men. The York court which tried him for murder, swayed by uncertainties, acquitted him, and he returned to Hull to a tumultuous welcome.

Both towns were embarrassed by the Quota Act of 1795, calculated to guarantee recruitment for the coming Napoleonic wars. York had to contribute 1,000 men annually, and Hull 731. Once more thieves were pressed. In 1807 Joshua Ashton of Patrington, convicted of stealing a handkerchief and a quantity of bacon, was despatched to the Royal Navy.

Opposition to the press gang was often full-blooded and ferocious. When a young Hull seaman was impressed in July 1815 the dock navvies overwhelmed the gang. The mayor, trying to read the Riot Act, was pulled down by his gold chain. A naval officer drawing his pistol was knocked down by a stone. Only when all local men were released did the vast crowd disperse. Finally, with the banishment of Napoleon to St Helena the long war ended, together with the need for pressed convicts.

chapter six

Capital Punishment

Hanging

In medieval times all authorities, including the Church, accepted hanging as an appropriate punishment. Indeed, in York the archbishop had a gallows on Foss Bridge and the dean and chapter hanged their felons out on the Haxby road, while the Knavesmire gallows erected in 1379 replaced that at Garrow Hill owned by St Mary's Abbey. The 'deadly evergreen' was indeed deadly – eventually – but few deaths were instantaneous. Much depended on the executioner's skill. The victim often writhed for several minutes. Even worse was the pulling away of a cart which left him half sprawled and slowly strangling until his weight choked him. Until William Marwood perfected his 'long drop' in mid-Victorian times, executioners resorted to pulling on the doomed man's legs.

The crime of rape was often a hanging matter. After Edward Hewison of the Earl of Northumberland's Light Horse was hanged in 1379 on the new Knavesmire Tyburn, his body was gibbeted (ie hung in chains and left to rot, as an awesome example) in the field where the offence had occurred.

Particular examples were made of pirates. In 1577 a number were captured off the Humber and tried by Earl Huntingdon, lord president of the North, assisted by Hull's mayor and aldermen. Thirteen were hanged and their corpses gibbeted along various parts of the Holderness coast.

Nor could highwaymen like Dick Turpin and Spence Broughton expect clemency. Notorious throughout Hallamshire, Broughton was tried for robbing the Sheffield-Rotherham mail of a single bill of exchange. Following his execution at York in 1792 his body was moved to Attercliffe Common, near the scene of the robbery, remaining on public view until 1827.

Capital offences included deer hunting, rabbit snaring, arson, and rescuing prisoners. Sometimes thieves were hanged. At York in 1775 John Vickers of Sheffield was hanged for taking foodstuffs and money; but magistrates could be reluctant to apply the noose for small larcenies.

Few cases were more pathetic than that of seventy-seven-year-old John Hoyland of Attercliff, hanged at York's Tyburn in 1793 on a charge of bestiality with an ass, on the doubtful testimony of two witnesses – both aggrieved employees.

Aram

The most serious capital crime, of course, has always been murder; and an eighteenth-century *cause celebre* still raising occasional controversy concerns Eugene Aram, born at Ramsgill (Nidderdale) in 1704 and son of a Ripley Castle gardener. He prospered, became a schoolmaster but fell under suspicion at the disappearance in 1741 of a somewhat dubious friend, Daniel Clark. Time passed and Aram moved to become a master at Kings Lynn Grammar School; and

Above left: Site of Knavesmire Tyburn, York.

Above right: Noose and Gibbet inn sign, Broughton Road, Sheffield.

Left: Eugene Aram.

Opposite page: Eugene Aram: the murder.

it was here that he was arrested after another former associate, Richard Houseman, had declared suddenly that Clark's body would be found in St Robert's Cave, Knaresborough. The poet Thomas Hood has described the arrest thus:

> Two stern faced men set out from Lynn
> Through the cold and heavy mist,
> And Eugene Aram walked between
> With gyves upon his wrist.

During protracted inquiries Aram was held in York Castle, preparing a scholarly defence. Despite his eloquence at the assizes the verdict went against him, and he was hanged on 6 August 1759. His body was then gibbeted just above Mother Shipton's Inn, Knaresborough – a raw spectacle for his widow and children.

Felons fall out

Another example of villains quarrelling was the Parker/Driscoll case. In February 1868 Dan Driscoll, a Londoner, and Fred Parker, a Hemingborough man, were freed from the Beverley House of Correction. After celebrating in a number of public houses in the Hemingborough area, Parker killed Driscoll, stealing his watch and escaping by the Ouse ferry to Drax. Here, in another hostelry, he was arrested trying to sell the watch. His execution on 4 April in the same year was the last on the Knavemire.

The Busby stoop chair

After dissensions over money, Thomas Busby murdered his father-in-law, Daniel Auty, with a hammer. Hanged at York in 1702, he was subsequently gibbeted on the gallows at Carlton Miniott crossroads. After his chair's removal to the Busby Stoop Inn, Sandhutton, several regulars, believed to have sat in it, died somewhat mysteriously. Nowadays at Thirsk Museum the item is suspended well out of reach of visitors!

The Grassington affair

The shock waves caused by the murder of one resident by another, and the latter's hanging and gibbeting, are certain to reverberate for many years in a small community. Such was the case with Tom Lee of Grassington. After killing Dr Richard Petty in Grass Wood he was hanged at York in 1768, and his corpse gibbeted on Donkey Hill for four years.

After Culloden

It was, of course, the broader political, social and industrial concerns that sometimes brought a spate of hangings. After the Scots' defeat at Culloden in 1746 retribution fell heavily on the Jacobite survivors: seventy-eight were transported to Antigua; forty-eight were pardoned, subject to service in George III's Hanoverian Regiment; and twenty-two were hanged at York Tyburn. Captain Hamilton's heart was carved out by the hangman and held aloft with the ritual cry, 'Behold, the heart of a traitor!' A few dextrous flourishes later, the cry went up, 'Behold, the four quarters of a traitor!' The heads of William Connolly and James Mayne were spiked on Micklegate Bar until they were stolen some years later by a Catholic, William Arundel, who was

Busby Stoop sign, Sandhutton.

Busby stoop chair, Sandhutton.

fined £5 and imprisoned for two years. A report of the executions concluded, 'The whole of the proceedings was conducted with the utmost decency and good order'.

With hanging, drawing and quartering, the prisoner was first hanged, cut down and disembowelled while still alive, then beheaded, and the body cut into quarters. The punishment was abolished in 1814.

Corn and coining

During the last part of the eighteenth century bread riots regularly broke out, and were taken seriously by the lord lieutenant and high sheriff, who were quick to bring in soldiers. In 1783 Thomas Spencer, once an accomplice of the notorious Cragg Vale coiners, led a mob to besiege the stores of Halifax corn merchants. For this offence he was hanged at York and gibbeted on Beacon Hill, overlooking the scene of the crime. Coin clipping at Cragg Vale, near Mythlmroyd, had resulted in many hangings, notably of the leader, David Hartley, in 1770.

Forgery and interference with the currency continued to bring the death sentence. In 1800 Elizabeth Johnson was hanged at York for forging a £1 bill.

Trouble at the mill

But it was the Luddite upheavals that brought the most dramatic industrial unrest and new policies in law and order. After mills were burnt down in Leeds and Horbury in the first months of 1812, a Luddite army (followers of a largely mythical General Ludd) numbering 150 and led by George Mellor attacked Rawfold's Mill at Liversedge on 11 April.

Their aim was to smash the shearing frames that threatened to displace hand labour. Marsden blacksmiths Enoch and James Taylor made the new frames, but a much older 'Enoch', the smith's hammer, would be used to smash them, hence the rallying cry, 'Enoch's made 'em an' Enoch'll break 'em!'

The mob was met by troops, musket fire and the mill owner, William Cartwright, who had been expecting trouble. Five men were wounded and Sam Hartley of Halifax was killed. William Booth of Huddersfield was fatally wounded and brought into the Star Inn to receive spiritual comfort from the Revd Hammond Robberson, a local vicar recruited by the authorities to find out what he could. Booth could play the same game. 'Can tha keep a secret?' he whispered. The man of God smiled encouragingly. Booth nodded and winced: 'Ha – Ah can, an' all!'

He might well have been mulling over George Mellor's future plans. On 28 April Mellor and friends shot a Marsden mill owner, William Horsfall, who admitted himself ready to 'ride up to his saddle girth in Luddite blood'. Ironically, he bled to death over two days.

Betrayals, disillusion and arrests followed. Mellor and sixteen accomplices were hanged at York (8 January 1813) and seven more were transported to Australia for administering illegal oaths.

These events contributed to a policy of repression by the Liverpool government. In 1817 the Habeas Corpus Act was suspended in order to delay particular judicial procedures; and two years later the Six Acts strengthened the powers of JPs to seize unlawful arms and put down sedition. These measures were short-lived, however, for within a few years Sir Robert Peel as a visionary home secretary reduced many penal measures, and went on to question the efficacy of amateur policing.

In due course two Yorkshire women were to portray the Luddite outbreaks in famous novels: *Shirley* by Charlotte Brontë and *Inheritance* by Phyllis Bentley. Serious disturbances continued into the 1840s with the Chartist protests. Mills were attacked and there was mob violence in the West Riding. In May 1848 a hostile crowd burst into the Bingley Petty Sessions, rescuing two indicted prisoners and threatening Squire Ferrand, JP.

Rawfold's Mill.

It is interesting to find names reappearing in other circumstances. An informer at the time of the Rawfold's Mill attack by the name of Joseph Ratcliffe, a wool cropper's apprentice, later prospered, becoming in 1846 the Halifax beadle, and mace bearer to the town's first mayor. Not that the mace conferred immunity: two years after making Leeds' new civic mace, Arthur Mountjoy, a Briggate goldsmith was found guilt of coining and was hanged at York.

Stitch-up case

The only public hanging at Armley took place in September 1864 when James Sargisson and Joe Myers were punished for separate murders. In an attempt to cheat the hangman Myers slit his own throat, but was stitched up again in order to fulfil his appointment. A crowd estimated at 10,000 – including mothers and babies – jostled and fought to watch the proceedings. Sargisson was seen to struggle for several minutes.

This incident, typical of many which brought revulsion to 'hanging matches' as a public spectacle, also brought considerable disorder; under the Capital Punishment Amendment Act (1868) all future executions were to be conducted within the prison walls, and in the presence of the sheriff, chaplain, gaoler and surgeon. The waiting public would witness only the raising of the black flag and the subsequent notice confirming death by hanging.

Whereas in 1819 there were in theory some 220 capital offences, by 1868 just four remained – murder, high treason, piracy and the destruction of arsenals and dockyards.

R.I.P.

Another noteworthy Armley hanging was of the notorious Sheffield burglar Charlie Peace by William Marwood on 25 February 1879; he was convicted at Leeds Assizes. The immediate

Execution of Sargisson and Myers. (courtesy of Leeds City Library)

charge was shooting the husband of a lady he had fancied. Years earlier he had shot a Manchester policeman, allowing another man, William Hebron, to suffer a life sentence. Finally he confessed to both murders, and Hebron was released. Despite his record, Peace was regarded as something of a folk hero, on account of his versatility as fiddler and roof-top escapist, spiced by amorous dalliances and regularly deceiving the law.

Place reminders

Scores of place names remind us that summary justice was hereabouts carried out: Gallows Hill, Skidby (near Hull), Brompton (NR), and Ripon. Variations include Gallows Lane (Beverley), Gallows Field, Howden, Gallowgate, Richmond. Gallows Dike retains its stone base near Whinny Nab/Saltergate, as does the site of Gallows Howe near Castleton. Then there are the 'gibbets', like Gibbet Hill, Farnham (near Knaresborough).

An end was made to gibbeting in 1839.

Rope cheats

Two Yorkshiremen survived the rope. Convicted of felony, John Bartendale was hanged on 27 March 1634 outside Micklegate Bar, York. Forty-five minutes later he was cut down, declared dead and was buried nearby. However, bystanders, seeing the soil move, scattered it with their bare hands and dug him free – restoratives were applied and he recovered. At York Assizes he was formally released, and enjoyed many more years as an ostler.

The second instance, too, was a very near thing. Fifteen minutes after the noose had tightened round the neck of a Malton burglar, John Smith, at the Knavesmire in 1705, a horseman galloped up, waving a reprieve. The victim was cut down, found to be breathing, was bled and medically treated – and thereafter was known as 'Half-hanged Smith'.

Two Yorkshire hangmen

William Currey of York, nicknamed 'Mutton' because of his former addiction to sheep stealing, was convicted in 1800 for an offence at Heworth, near York. While awaiting transportation he was offered the job of hangman – a situation not unprecedented, as vacancies rarely drew many applicants. He fulfilled the role for thirty-five years, though not without controversy. He was responsible for despatching George Mellor and other Luddites in 1813. But alcohol, far from steadying his nerve, made him prone to error; on one occasion he dropped his noose around

Charlie Peace: sketch by Frank Lockwood during trial.

Charlie Peace shooting Constable Robinson.

Charlie Peace's tools.

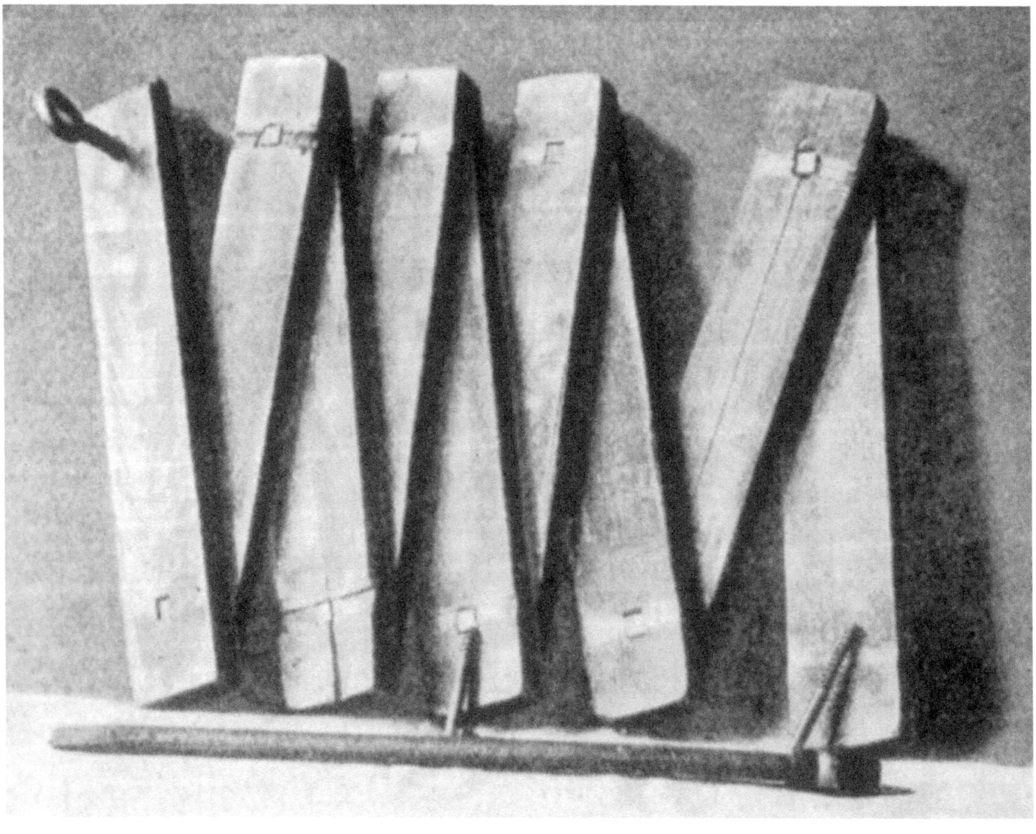

Folding ladder and crowbar used by Charles Peace.

Right: Charles Peace.

Below: The name 'Gallows Lane' dates from the mid-sixteenth century, and probably refers to the Archbishop's scaffold in Beverley.

the neck of the officiating chaplain. One particular hanging, that of William Brown in 1821, was so botched that an incensed crowd attacked him on the way home. Currey died in Thirsk workhouse in 1841.

A former Bradford policeman, James Berry (1852-1913) also acquired a soubriquet – 'the Reluctant Hangman' – succeeding the redoubtable William Marwood (he of 'the long drop') in 1884. During his eight years in office Berry was responsible for over 134 hangings. Later, however, as well as working as a music-hall entertainer, he campaigned against the death penalty, arguing that it was unchristian and posed no noticeable deterrent. An account of his *Experiences as an Executioner* appeared in 1892.

Gallows humour

One example, from 1690, must suffice. William Barwick of Cawood, having drowned his wife in a pond, told the hangman he hoped the rope wouldn't break and drop him, as he didn't want to finish up a cripple for life. The man in black reassured him (naturally!), a tale that had doubtless been repeated for decades – and too often afterwards!

Hand of glory

On a more macabre note it used to be thought that a dead criminal's hand, hacked off at night, properly pickled with fat from the gibbeted corpse, and primed with a lit candle, could confer immunity from arrest. Such was the 'Hand of Glory'. Pursuers would be immobilised, encouraging villains in their chorus:

> O Hand of Glory, shed thy light:
> Direct us to our spoil tonight.

James Berry, 'the Reluctant Hangman'.

One such gruesome hand, relic of a brutal but credulous age, may still be seen at the Pannett Park Museum, Whitby. It is thought to derive from Hawthorn Cottage in Eskdale in the early nineteenth century.

Dick and Swift Nick

Captured at the Green Dragon Inn, Welton, this most notorious highwayman was soon transferred to York Castle from the Beverley House of Correction. These were the days when horse stealing was a capital offence; accordingly Turpin's conviction was certain. As a final histrionic gesture he threw himself off the Knavesmire scaffold, and was buried on the same day, 7 April 1739, in St George of the Beanhills churchyard.

It now seems likely that Nick Nevison, not Dick Turpin, made the legendary ride to York from Gad's Hill, near Rochester, to establish an alibi, upheld in court, after a highway robbery. Charles II dubbed him 'Swift Nick'. After many further brushes with the law he was arrested at the Magpie Inn at Sandal for a murder at North Elmshall in 1681, having subsequently dared to walk the streets of Wakefield. Executed at the Knavesmire on 15 March 1684 he was buried in St Mary's churchyard, Castlegate. Audacious, good humoured – charitable – even, he has been seen as a romantic figure and engaging trickster permanently fixed in West Riding mythology.

The Yorkshire witch

Mary Bateman had a record of parting the gullible from their money via health panaceas. A familiar stratagem was to beg a few guinea coins supposedly to sew into the patient's bed linen in order to promote recovery. After his wife, Rebecca, died of poisoning, William Perigo of Bramley opened the covers to find only paper and small coins. The penny had dropped! Bateman was arrested, put in York Castle, convicted of administering the poison, and went to the scaffold on 20 March 1809. In vain the watching crowd waited for an escape trick. Her body was conveyed to Leeds General Infirmary for the customary dissection. Such was the morbid curiosity of the public that the corpse was exhibited at threepence a time, and samples of skin sold. Her skeleton remains in the Thackray Medical Museum.

Another controversial hanging was that of Ethel Major, the only woman to be hanged in Hull Prison – on 19 December 1934. Her crime was to have poisoned her husband after experimenting on a dog. There have been a number of claims, by prisoners and staff, to have seen her ghost!

Beheading

As a less shameful death than hanging, beheading was practised by the Normans when aristocratic heads had to roll.

During the War of the Roses, started by Richard of York to dethrone the Lancastrian King Henry VI, reprisals often resulted in noble beheadings. After the Battle of Wakefield Green, fought in a snowstorm on 30 December 1460, Richard was found to the rear of his outnumbered and defeated army. His fate was determined by the bloody-minded Queen Margaret, in Shakespeare's memorable words: 'Off with his head and set it on York gates/So York may overlook the town of York'. (*Henry VI*, Part III.I.IV).

So Richard's severed head, mounted with a gold paper crown, was spiked on Micklegate Bar, along with the Earl of Salisbury's and other nobles. A reversal of fortunes was marked by the most terrible Battle of Towton, fought on Palm Sunday, 1461. 'No prisoner and no quarter!' was

Above: Turpin's headstone, St George of the Beanhills church, York.

Left: Mary Bateman, 'the Yorkshire Witch'.

Mary Evans, who was hanged at York in August 1799. (courtesy of York City Art Gallery)

the order of Edward, Richard's eldest son, already proclaimed as the future Edward IV, and now determined to wreak vengeance on the Lancastrians. It was said that the Cock Beck stream ran with blood, and a crimson trail led all the way to York. 'Butcher' Clifford, lord of Skipton Castle, fell, and the Yorkist heads on Micklegate were replaced by Lancastrian ones, including the Earl of Devonshire, Sir Baldwin Fulford, Lord Kyme and Sir William Hall.

Another noteworthy reversal took place at Scarborough Castle after an astonishing takeover. On 24 March 1557, an otherwise uneventful market day, Sir Thomas Stafford, furious at the recent marriage of Catholic Queen Mary to Philip of Spain, disguised thirty followers as peasants, strolled into the castle – and effected a bloodless coup. Thus arose the expression, 'The Scarborough Warning', or a word and a blow – but the blow comes first! Retaliation was swift and inevitable. The Earl of Westmoreland was sent to recover the castle, and Stafford was beheaded.

A royalist judged to have been implicated in a number of Civil War plots was Sir Henry Slingsby, who after the battle of Marston Moor in 1644 hid away in his own rafters at the Red House, near Moor Monkton. Eventually betrayed, he was dragged out by Roundhead soldiers to be beheaded in 1658. His body lies beneath a black marble slab in Knaresborough parish church; the shirt he wore at his execution is displayed in the Old Courthouse Museum.

Another reminder of military justice is an embellished plaque on the south wall of St Mary's church, Beverley. Immediately prior to Christmas 1689, Johannes Frederick Bellow was beheaded in the market place for killing a comrade in a duel. As members of a company recruited by William of Orange to fight in Ireland, they could have fallen out over any matter – women, money, personal grievance. We do not know.

Micklegate Bar, York.

The Sharp Maiden

What is certain is that by the middle of the seventeenth century the 'Sharp Maiden' of Halifax was still a fearful sanction. Between 1541 and 1650 forty-nine persons were guillotined, six of them women, plus a father and daughter. The first victim was believed to be John of Dalton in 1286, executed under the ancient custom of *Ingfanthief*, whereby the overlord, within his Liberty, could bring to trial and summarily punish any thief caught red-handed or confessing to a felony. During the fourteenth century the gibbet (guillotine) had largely disappeared from Yorkshire, apart from some isolated instances, as at Wakefield.

But this form of public beheading continued at Halifax (Cow Green, later Gibbet Street), aimed especially at wool thieves. Cloth left to dry outside on tenter frames, for example, was a temptation. Animal thefts, too, sometimes brought the full weight of the blade on the offender's neck. In theory any item valued at more than thirteen pence could, if stolen, bring the thief to the scaffold. Halifax had its own litany, attributed to John Taylor:

> At Halifax the Law so sharp doth deal
> That whoso more than thirteen pence doth steal
> They have a Tyn that wondrous quick and well
> Sends thieves all headless into Heaven and Hell.

Danish soldiers' plaque, St Mary's church, Beverley.

Immediately before execution the victim was seated in nearby stocks with the stolen goods hanging around his neck, or otherwise displayed in front of him.

When all was ready he was led onto the scaffold to the melancholy accompaniment of drum and bagpipes. The stone platform supported a pair of stout wooden uprights some 15ft tall, grooved on the inside to allow the 8lb axe to move freely up and down. With the sacrifice bound and recumbent, there were prayers and comfortable words from Psalm 4:8 – 'I will lay me down in peace and sleep; for Thou Lord only makest me dwell in safety'. A raised finger from the town bailiff signalled the removal of the securing pin under the axe. The trailing rope was pulled hard – or, if the stolen animal had been recovered, it was harnessed to advance so as to jerk out the pin. Piquant justice indeed! After the oohs and aahs from the crowd, the block was raised by cord and pulley.

Universal awe of the Halifax gibbet has given rise to the Thieves' Litany – 'From Hell, Hull and Halifax Good Lord deliver us!' Hell conjured up visions of eternal damnation; Hull was to be avoided – even beggars had to work there, disturbingly near the riverside gallows; and Halifax had the gibbet!

It is claimed that only one man ever escaped the 'wondrous Tyn'. Somehow eluding the axe fall, John Lacy ran across the town boundary and lived away for seven years. But on returning he was arrested and executed on 29 January 1623. A public house, the Running Man on Pellon Lane commemorates the event.

While for most folk the gibbet was an object of mortal dread – lesser offenders were sometimes nailed to it by their ears – the army had no use for it. When two Parliamentary soldiers deserted and were recaptured at Halifax they were hanged on a gallows specially erected (January 1643) near the gibbet.

The last two victims, John Wilkinson and Anthony Mitchell, both of Sowerby, were convicted of the theft of Kersey cloth and two horses. They were buried in the parish churchyard. This double event proved too much for the people of Halifax, and guillotining was stopped in 1650 as being too barbarous. The original 10in blade survives in the Industrial Museum, and the gibbet has been re-erected on its former site in Gibbet Street, having been unearthed in 1839 during ground clearance.

Burning

Of all forms of execution, burning must surely rank among the most horrific. The Reformation claimed many martyrs by this means. Richard and John Snell, Protestants of Bedale, were burned in Richmond market place in 1558.

Apart from religious victims there were two main categories sometimes deemed flame-worthy. The first crime was witchcraft. While many witches were hanged rather than burned, there were two exceptions from seventeenth-century Pocklington: in 1631, Old Wife Green was dragged from her cottage by a mob and bound to a stake in the market square; the case of Isabella Billington differed in that there was a substantiated murder charge to answer, that of her mother, whom she had crucified. After hanging, her body was burned at York in 1649.

Secondly, until the close of the eighteenth century women could be charged with 'petty treason', i.e. murdering their husbands. Burning, it was then argued, was somehow milder than hanging: more purifying, less brutal. Nevertheless, the executioner generally believed it humane to strangle his client first. This happened to Mary Ellah of Broomfleet on the Humber, executed at Tyburn in 1757 for strangling her husband. In 1776 when a Flamborough woman, Elizabeth Boardingham, was convicted in York for 'petty treason' – in this case poisoning her man – the judge granted a measure of leniency: 'the law has allowed some mitigation and first you are to be strangled at a stake

Halifax gibbet.

Snell plaque, Richmond.

and then burned by fire'. Ann Sowerby of Whitby, executed at Tyburn in 1767 for having included arsenic in her husband's breakfast curds, was also granted this small mercy. She was drawn on a hurdle and throttled with the hangman's rope, so that she was already dead before being roasted – all in public view. The burning of women murderers was not abolished until 1789.

Pressing

Pressing to death ('*peine forte et dure*') was once the fate of accused persons refusing to plead, often to prevent their estates being confiscated. It was a torture deliberately prolonged. The body was laid down and increasingly piled with layers of boards and stones. Bread and water were offered on alternate days, and the victim was repeatedly invited to plead.

Up to 1772 trial could not proceed without a plea of guilty or not guilty. Continuing uncertainties were finally resolved by an Act of 1827 by which the courts entered a plea of not guilty in the event of a refusal from the dock.

Two celebrated cases occurred in Yorkshire within a generation. The first was Margaret Clitherow, daughter of a wealthy butcher in York's Shambles. Between 1577 and 1584, when recusancy was treasonable, she was several times imprisoned for giving children Catholic teaching and allowing Mass to be said in her home. In 1586, having already served ten days in the Ouse Bridge prison for similar offences, she refused to plead before a Guildhall Quarter Sessions over a charge of sheltering a Catholic priest. Such a disclosure might come to involve others – an odd thought, considering that her stepfather, Henry May, Lord Mayor of York, was rounding up other recusants.

Margaret Clitherow.

She died under pressure of doors and weights in the toll booth. According to one legend, two beggars were paid for this work. John, her husband, was banished. The authorities, recognising a sensitive issue, had offered leniency on grounds of possible pregnancy – but this, too, was refused. A shrine to the Blessed Margaret, who was canonised in 1970, is situated at 36 The Shambles; and her mummified hand rests at the Bar Convent in Blossom Street.

The second famous refusal to plead was by Walter Calverley, lord of the manor of Calverley Old Hall, near Bradford. Family quarrels resulted in the stabbing of his two sons, William and Walter. He was pressed to death in York Castle in 1605.

Shooting
There is little evidence of the bullet being used as a legalised form of capital punishment, except, perhaps, through military intervention. It remains true that during riots (for example Luddite, or Reform Bill agitation in Sheffield, 1832) a number of citizens were shot by soldiers, but these were responses to civil disobedience, and not penalties determined in courts of law. Firing squads were known, however, during the Civil War. All Saints church, Ripley (NR) has bullet marks embedded on its east wall, allegedly made by Roundheads executing Royalist prisoners after Marston Moor, 1644. When Oliver Cromwell insisted on imposing himself overnight in Ripley Castle, Lady Ingilby sat up throughout on guard with a pair of cocked pistols – the second, she assured him, in case she missed with the first!

chapter seven

Chiding Children

Schooling

The upbringing of children has necessarily involved some balance of rewards and punishments – 'the carrot and the stick'. Corporal punishment in schools was not banned until 1986. 'Spare the road and spoil the child,' as proverbial wisdom has it.

At the village school in Masham in 1818 parents were required to accept any punishment that the headteacher thought proper for their children, who would otherwise be expelled.

Particularly vulnerable were orphans. The workhouse foundlings at the Pateley Bridge Union Workhouse in mid-Victorian times were, perhaps, better treated than many – though official accounts must be read with caution. Corporal punishment was said to be rare, but offences like name calling, nuisance behaviour, singing disapproved songs, breakages etc led to isolation and reduced diets. One can but speculate on the circumstances that led to the stealing of coal.

The Sailors' Orphans Home in Hull was by no means alone in finding bed-wetting a persistent problem. Some offenders were caned and made to wear black armbands bearing the letters WB. For others, the forced drinking of cabbage water was thought to be a satisfactory remedy. Periods of strict silence were insisted on during meals and at bedtimes. Boys brought up in an ambience of marching and saluting the flag were well primed for careers in the Army and Navy.

We need to remember that early generations of elementary pupils and parents were largely unused to habits of book learning, obedience – and sometimes cleanliness. George Grubb, head of Hawes School between 1879 and 1904, often had a class of 100 pupils. Individual treatment was rarely possible and justice might be rough. Children were required to sit up and listen, with backs straight and arms folded to avoid fidgeting. Some West Riding schools devised wooden finger stocks, and in some instances a stocked hand might be tied behind the child's back.

Considerable feats of memory were demanded with multiplication tables, parts of speech, Kings and battles, capes and bays etc, with little understanding thereof. From 1862 – the era of 'payment by results' – part of the school's income depended on various standards being achieved to the satisfaction of Her Majesty's Inspectors.

Discipline was frequently severe, at least for boys, who gave most trouble. Girls tended to be more compliant, though verbal humiliations, shakings, smacks and standing in a corner were not unknown. In the Wesleyan Chapel at Netherthong, near Holmfirth, a stone is inscribed, 'In memory of Ann Hobson, aged 12 years, who died through fear of whipping by the schoolmistress in 1856'. A Selby girls' academy sometimes resorted to restraining a pupil by requiring her to stand with her back to a kind of fixed yoke, her arms outstretched on the handles.

From 1870 some school boards, like Sheffield's, declared that only headteachers were to administer corporal punishment, which was to be reasonable, moderate and by use of an approved cane. But such regulations were almost universally flouted. Joseph Lister was sacked

Victorian finger stocks. (courtesy of Bankfield Museum, Halifax)

from Staxton School in 1880 after various complaints had been made, including striking a girl on the head with a cane.

Teachers of an older generation will confirm that there are infinite gradations of physical chastisement between, say, the slightest hand pressure and a full-blooded swipe. To modern youngsters it is hard to convey the formidable range of tortures suffered by their elders as children. No list could be exhaustive, but would have to include the strap; the slipper; a repeated tattoo across the knuckles with a ruler's edge; a sharp smack across the face, or various slaps about the body with alternate hands; boxed ears; head beaten with a book; assaults with a blackboard ruler; being struck by missiles like chalk or blackboard rubber; rough handling, shakings, pushing, felling; pinching, kicks, being picked up bodily and dropped. At the National School, Pocklington, the master sometimes consigned a boy to the churchyard stocks.

Talkative children were sometimes gagged, or made to sit with a handkerchief or duster over their mouths. At Eccleshall CE School, the master, Mr Wainwright, was accused in 1866 of depriving scholars of their lunches.

All this is to say nothing of canings, which had the benefit of legal recognition. One apocryphal account has linked the cane with sweetmeat rewards. In Tudor times a Pontefract schoolmaster, finding on the seashore branches left by Spanish vessels, took home a sample of the whippy canes. Alas, says the story, these instruments proved brittle in use, and when pieces fell off, pupils found them to their taste… thus were Pontefract cakes discovered!

A more recent and plausible anecdote tells of late Victorian masters in Barnsley experimenting to maximise the impact of a wielded cane by cutting into its lower part and weaving into the gaps a thin but vicious twine. All too often caning was overdone, and the master regretted an over-hasty reaction, or tried to explain away a punishment. Thus we read of an incident in 1891 at Aldbrough School, on the Holderness coast. In the words of the headmaster, William Fell:

W.E. Forster, MP for Bradford. His Education Act, 1870 enabled board schools to supplement the elementary schools provided by the religious societies – a major step towards making education compulsory.

The cane broke in two at the first stroke on his back. I gave him four strokes on the back with the short piece of cane and one on the hand. On moving his hand I caught the back of his fingers and one finger is marked.

Tougher young spirits refused the rod, or even snatched it and deliberately broke it. Tension between home and school frequently resulted in parental visits to exact retribution on an over-zealous master.

Many teachers saw no fine line between ignorance and laziness, and the cane was sometimes used to motivate the dull and the slothful. In some instances it probably worked!

Truancy also was severely punished, as from Victorian times pupil attendance affected the government grant and hence teachers' salaries. Apart from being beaten, truants were sometimes stood on a stool for a while, holding a book or a stone above their heads; or a log might be hung around their necks.

Some accounts tell of truants carted around the playground to be scorned, hissed, abused, shackled to a desk or paraded in a paper hat. Hunt days raised awkward issues, as few masters would deliberately antagonise the red-coated elite, so the obvious compromise was to arrange for the school to witness the hunt start. Unfortunately, absences requested by parents were legion – hirings, harvest, visit of a circus, looking after younger children, brambling (blackberrying), grandparents' illness, chopping thistles, helping the carrier and much more. Bullying was, and is, a reason for 'twagging'. It is surprising to find that at Cropton (NR) in the 1760s even the future whaling captain and Arctic explorer William Scoresby senior received rough treatment in the playground.

In Victorian times at Long Riston School (ER), Dicky Fewson created a system of pulleys, ropes and a basket by which naughty boys could be hauled up to the ceiling, there to hover and ponder their sins. 'Every pupil is given the chance to rise', was Dick's arch boast. Another option was to make a boy hang from a low beam by both arms in order to receive a thrashing.

Truant's clog used at Mount School, Whitby up to 1874. (courtesy of Whitby Literary and Philosophical Society)

Battles of wills, bluff and counter-bluff have always been aspects of psychological warfare between home and school. The following log-book entry dated 1882 for Haddesley School (NR) illustrates the point:

> William Whittaker brought an abusive letter from his mother because her boy had been sent home for his money. She informed me that she would not send the money until she thought proper. I sent both boys home until it was paid. It was – four days later.

Unfortunately, children were so often caught in the crossfire. It is hardly to be wondered that after such humiliations as being kept in, made to wear a dunce's cap or a derogatory label, youngsters longed to 'get one across' their persecutors. Hence so many anecdotes of hiding Sir's equipment, especially cane or chalk, putting glue on his chair, spiking the staffroom kettle or deliberately playing him up in front of visitors. Yet it needs to be stressed that very many enlightened teachers well understood that a firm, fair, good-humoured relationship dramatically reduced the need for more than the occasional sanction.

Grammar schools

It might be supposed that grammar schools would offer more sweetness and light, but they too were, in general, no-nonsense institutions. It is an interesting reflection that, centuries ago, masters graduating at university were ritually given a rod to display their competence by beating a boy publicly, the 'whipping boy' being compensated later. Grammar-school men soaked their birch twigs in brine to make them supple. Delinquents were made to fetch the birch and to kiss it as a sign of submission.

For centuries detailed rules had been laid down for floggings and expulsions. At Pontefract Boys Free Grammar School, founded by Edward VI in 1549, censures, punishments and rewards were wholly at the headmaster's discretion. Public 'adminitions' were commonplace, though cruelty or excessive punishment could bring an appeal to the mayor. At Heath Grammar School, Halifax, founded in 1585, a statute of 1730 insisted that scholars careless of dress, words, deeds, long hair or dirt would be severely punished, and on a second occasion expelled. Giggleswick School, a 1592 foundation, ruled that scholars negligent of learning were to be returned to their friends, to be brought up in some other honest trade. In common with many other enlightened seats of learning, new boys were uplifted and 'bumped'.

Truancy brought severe reprimands, beatings and ultimately expulsion, as was made clear at King James School, Knaresborough, of 1616 foundation, where boys were to provide their own bows and arrows for target practice. Woe betide any boy who came 'uncombed, unwashed, ragged or slovenly' for a brisk start at 6 a.m. in summer and 7 a.m. in winter.

Nor was there mollycoddling at the Society of Friends' School, Ackworth (founded 1779). Early rising, cold water washes, study, prayer and decorum were reinforced, as necessary, by periods of solitary confinement and beatings. The culprit's hands were tied and he was frogmarched away to await the principal, standing to attention, and displaying a label proclaiming his crime. Significant, perhaps, is the fact that among the interests of the founder, Dr John Fothergill, was prison reform.

Imaginative methods were taken a step further at Threshfield, near Grassington, a seventeenth-century establishment, where errants were stood on one leg while holding a heavy weight, like a small log, to which was pinned an improving homily which had to be learned by heart. On one occasion in later Victorian times a boy who stole blackcurrants from the master's garden was made to sew them back on again! The dunce's cap, the unkind placards, the solitary detentions, the ritual humiliations featured in the admonitory repertoire of Samuel Parker, headmaster of Woodhouse Grove School, a Bradford Methodist foundation, in the 1820s. A favourite witticism was to shout 'Nobody's at home!' as he tattooed his knuckles against a hapless boy's skull.

But some regulations were also meant to keep the staff in line. Under the procedures for the master or chaplain at the foundation in 1548 of Skipton Grammar School, a psalm and a prayer, '*Misere mei Deus*', were not to be omitted under penalty of 20d per day. Omissions could result in dismissal. The master had to attend the parish church on Sundays, under pain of 20s for a first

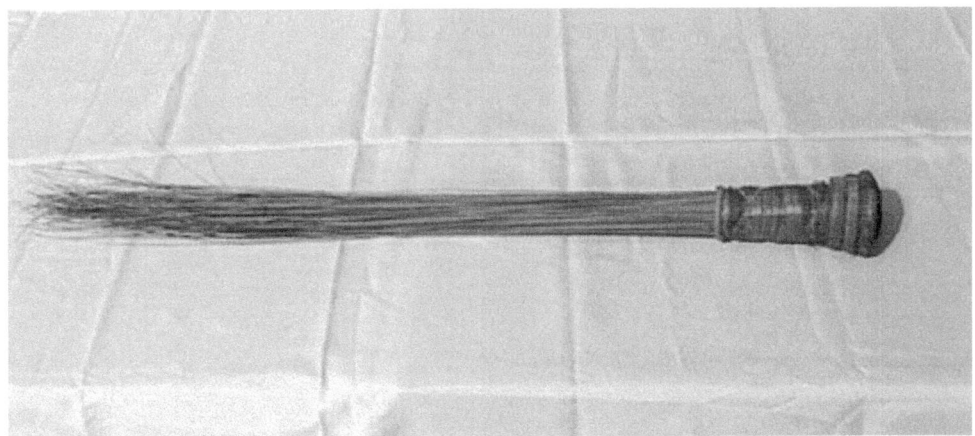

Birch used in private school, Whitby. (courtesy of Whitby Literary and Philosophical Society)

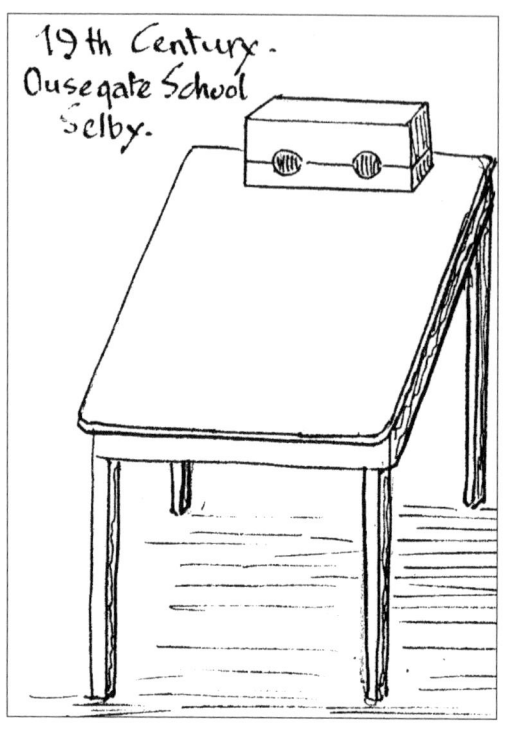

Punishment table. (courtesy of Selby Library)

absence, then 30s with dismissal. It is interesting to speculate on the changes that might have been brought about at this school had John Wesley been successful in his headship application.

Towards the end of the seventeenth century Burneston School (near Bedale) was concerned that the master should not be 'barred out' (locked out), as was the custom in many places. If this happened he was to send for the parents to command the boys to desist. Additional penalties militated against family men. The master appointed was to be childless, 'lest he bring a charge upon the parish.' And if he married, 'let him quit his place and his salary cease'.

The barring-out custom seems to have put some masters in a considerable quandary. Effectively done, it placed the man in a humiliating position, vis-à-vis parents, governing committees and, of course, the boys. In 1662 at Hull Grammar School the annual Martinmas ceremony (11 November) obliged the master to make no punishments, 'no rodds and ferrules' up to Christmas. Perhaps the wonder is that barring out didn't happen more often!

Mills and Factories

As the Industrial Revolution gained pace, controversy grew over their treatment of youngsters working in confined spaces for long hours. In 1830 Richard Oastler, later known as the Factory King, sent his first letter to the *Leeds Mercury*, on the emotive subject of slavery in Yorkshire:

> The very streets of our towns are every morning wet with the tears of innocent victims at the accursed shrine of avarice who are compelled not by the cart whip of the negro slave driver but by the dread of the equally appalling thong or strap of the overseer to hasten half-dressed but not half-fed children to those magazines of British infantile slavery, the worsted mills of the town of Bradford.

Richard Oastler, the Factory King.

His reference to the plight of the Negro was shrewdly calculated. William Wilberforce, born in Hull, for decades as a Yorkshire MP fought to free black slaves; meanwhile, young white slaves at home were sometimes breadwinners from as early as seven or eight years of age, working up to fifteen hours a day. Meals were snatched on the hoof. Fathers carried their sleeping offspring to and from the mills. At Walker and Edmonson's of Hebden Bridge, the foreman did not stop his cotton looms for breakfast, and a child's working week could be as long as seventy-seven hours.

The Report of the Factory Inquiry Commission in 1833 showed that Sam Rhodes, aged six, working in Mitchell's Worsted Mill, Keighley had been beaten with 'a strap with nails in it'. William Kershaw of Gomersal had been struck with a billy roller (a heavy iron bar) until he vomited blood. The day after his mother's irate visit to blacken the overseer's eye, William was beaten again for telling. It was further pointed out that mill girls were sometimes flogged with thonged whips, and worked longer hours than felons on prison hulks. Rosetta Baker, a ten-year-old spinner at Leach and Cousen's Mill, Bradford commonly worked from 6 a.m. until 7 p.m.: 'The overlooker brays (hits) us if we don't do our work, with his hands over the head'.

Other juvenile workers were repeatedly struck for alleged misdeeds. Boys were thrashed with the 'cat', a rope of four tails, until they screamed. Ears were torn. Children were rapped with bobbins or dragged by the hair. Heads were broken and calls of nature ignored.

Samuel Cooke testified that he had begun work at the age of seven at William Woodhead's, where he spent at least fifteen hours a day. When his head had been broken with a billy roller, and his mother complained to the 'slubbers' (card winders), they replied that if she didn't like it she could take him away. But Sam's efforts were essential for the maintenance of the family. Having received no schooling, he was illiterate.

A fifteen-year-old boy working in a Bradford worsted mill from the age of five, and used to working fifteen hours a day, now had permanently bent knees through standing for so long. The crooking of his left arm to hold cardings had resulted in another distorted limb.

John Hannam said of Wreaks Cotton Mill (Nidd Valley, four miles north of Ripley): 'The manager I have known start from one end of the room beating them and scarcely miss one.' Joseph Holmes reported: 'I used to get brayed over the ear at Fawcett's. I can't hear so well wi' it'.

The son of pauper parents, Robert Collyer was a bobbin doffer at Westhouse Mill in the Washburn Valley. Doffers took off full bobbins from the spinning frames and replaced them with empty ones. He had often been beaten with a strap. Some of his friends, doubled over their machines, never quite straightened up.

At Metcalfe's Mill, which worked flax at Glasshouses, Nidderdale, the Commission found that youngsters worked from 6 a.m. to 7 p.m. for five days a week, and two hours less on Saturdays. The firm employed no child under ten and claimed not to use corporal punishment. While this regime seemed less harsh, time was still money. Wages were cut for late arrivals and breakfast and drinks (provided by the workers) were taken while working. It was common practice here, as elsewhere, for the gateman to fine latecomers one penny; they were said to enter by 'penny-oil' (hole). Fines were also imposed for deviations like horseplay, pulling faces and teasing.

Accidents were legion, especially towards the end of a shift, when the young workers were refreshed by dashes of cold water, or enforced pinches of snuff to make them sneeze. Hazardous indeed was the lot of the Dewsbury 'piecers', who mended broken threads on the spinning mules of the 'shoddy' trade by crawling under moving machinery. On the eastern edge of Kirkheaton churchyard stands a column over a grave for seventeen girls aged between ten and fourteen who were accidentally burnt to death in 1818 whilst on night work at Atkinson's Cotton Mill by the Colne Bridge.

As the evidence piled up, revealing the stark horror of conditions endured by mill and factory children, so increased the momentum for change. John Wood, a Bradford mill owner, joined forces with Oastler. During a Commons speech for the great Factory Bill, Michael Sadler emphasised his words by producing a heavy leather strap of the kind used by Yorkshire mill overseers, and cracking it down on the table in front of him.

Success crowned their efforts in 1833 – in the same year that Wilberforce, on his deathbed, heard of the long-awaited measure to free black slaves. Henceforward, no children under nine were to work in factories and mills; nine to thirteen year olds were to labour no more than nine hours a day; and thirteen to eighteen year olds a maximum of twelve hours. Although the principle of inspection was conceded, some years were to pass before it took effect and too often children were hidden out of sight when the inspector called. The next step was to reduce working hours to ten a day, which was achieved in 1847.

Meantime the personal fortune of Richard Oastler took a downturn. Sacked as steward of Fixby Hall, Huddersfield in 1840, he was sent to the Fleet Prison for debt, but continued his campaign there for three years in the *Fleet Papers*. In 1844 he made a triumphant return to the West Riding. He died in Harrogate in 1861, an immortal in the annals of factory reform.

In Sheffield young apprentices in the various branches of cutlery trades seemed to fare better. Few witnesses reported to the Children's Employment Commission, 1843 of unduly harsh treatment. Cellar boys at the Abbeydale Works, which specialised in scythe manufacture, worked long and often uncomfortable hours overnight, and up to about 1850 were exposed to open machinery. They were at general beck and call but some of their tasks, like carrying beer to their elders, were actively appreciated. Walter Wilkinson, apprenticed to a cutlery firm, wrote to his sister in 1826:

> I am at the call of everyone in the house and has my victuals measured like a dog and am fit for nothing but to get manure into the garden. I am called all the foul names that can ever be mentioned, and must do all the dirty jobs about the place.

This was apt to be the lot of 'bun' (bound) apprentices to the 'Little Mesters', small family firms making knives and edged tools. They might be clipped, kicked, punched and cursed while serving their time, but unlike the young slaves in mills and factories they could eventually hope for reasonable livelihoods, possibly becoming masters themselves.

Factory Acts could abolish the most obvious physical abuses, but mill owners obsessed with cost cutting were given to exploitation. A new opportunity of recruiting vulnerable young people came in 1846 with numbers of Irish families flocking to Bradford to escape from the catastrophic potato famine. In Thomas Lach's Birkshead Mill, Wilsden, these 'Tipperary orphans' were hard-driven, pushed around and allocated the worst jobs... but at least they survived.

Yet there were some exemplary employers. At Bingley, Titus Salt built Saltaire, and at Halifax Edward Akroyd built Akroydon – model communities which demonstrated that industrial prosperity could be combined with humanity and decency.

For eight to thirteen year olds, compulsory schooling of three hours per day had been written into the Factory Act of 1844, thus establishing the half-time system. Children did alternating weekly shifts, working in the morning and attending afternoon classes, this order being reversed the following week. In 1917 Halifax still had 1,000 half-timers. While factory girls continued, sometimes, to be rapped smartly with a stick if their attention wandered from their looms, school discipline grew irksome on youngsters, especially boys, who were also wage earners – and premature adults. Some became rebellious, bringing on themselves the customary sanctions, including expulsion. But the system lingered until 1922.

Mines

Up to the 1840s child labour was exploited in the coal mines of the West Riding. The Children's Employment Commission painted an unhappy picture:

> Chained, belted, harnessed like dogs in a go-cart, black, saturated with wet and more than half-naked, crawling upon their hands and feet, and dragging their heavy loads behind them – they present an appearance indescribably disgusting and unnatural. (First Report, Appendix; Part ii, 1842, page 75).

J.C. Symons, Parliamentary Commissioner commented:

> One of the most disgusting sights I have ever seen was that of young females, dressed like boys in trousers, crawling on all fours with belts round their waists, and chains passing between their legs at day pits at Hunshelf Bank and in many small pits near Holmfirth and New Mill.

Trappers as young as five and six 'sat in small holes with a string in their little hands, in darkness and solitude, for twelve hours or more at a stretch.' Every few minutes when a corve (truck) was trundled through the tunnel, the string was pulled to open the ventilation doors. At four years of age Thomas Townsend had been brought from Batley workhouse as a trapper at Thornhill Colliery. And it was generally the workhouse 'apprentices' that came in for most punishment. In the commissioners' words, 'These lads are made to go where other men will not let their children go... if they will not do it, they take them to the magistrates who commit them to prison.'

Then again, there was some suggestion that some fathers came down heaviest on beating their own sons. Beating was 'the means whereby children are kept to their work – and the punishment of bad language and misconduct'. One lad admitted to getting 'a bit of pick-shaft'. John Roper, twelve, of Deep Pits Colliery, Sheffield, said, 'Sometimes they beat me when I leave the corves off... but I'd rather be in the pit than go to school.' A thoughtful stance for enlightened minds to ponder.

Young Roper was a harrier who pushed loaded corves (up to 8cw) from the coalface to the shaft bottom, negotiating some 'gates' less than 2ft high. Fearful cruelties were perpetrated. Children were kicked and had missiles thrown at them. Escape was impossible. William Higgins, the product of a Liverpool reformatory, a harrier at Hartshead Moor, after chastisement managed to hide away for three days in a 'gob-hole', eating leftover candles. Females were constantly at risk from sexual abuse.

As with the Factory Commission a decade earlier, evidence of the most hellish working conditions, cruelty and savage punishment were overwhelming. The Mines Act of 1842, forbidding the employment underground of women, or boys below ten, took time to implement, as only one inspector was initially appointed. Some lads even above ground were saddled with awesome responsibilities. In 1853 at Liversedge Colliery a mere twelve year old described as a 'winding engineman', charged with drawing the pit cage up and down, fell into his machinery and was killed. Amongst historic accidents was that at the Huskar Colliery in 1838, when twenty-six children were drowned.

Less publicised has been the employment of children in the lead mines of Swaledale, Arkengarthdale, Wensleydale and Nidderdale up to the mid-nineteenth century. Boys of ten or twelve dragged loaded hoppers onto the dressing floor, where, alongside women, they broke up the ore and waste with hammers; or, on the 'weshin rake', they washed and sieved the ore ready for smelting. Up to the 1840s some, the 'Windy Kings', were employed underground, working hand-operated fans. Others loaded ore boxes from a bucket attached to a shoulder harness, or did odd jobs like crawling up the smelt mill flues to scrape off encrusted carbon deposits. Slackers were not tolerated, and overmen could be harsh in summary punishment. A favourite trick was to thrust lads' heads into a tub of cold water.

Living in these macho communities, boys were bred to be tough. Booze in Swaledale, despite its name, never had a pub, but many were the fights with Langthwaite men. Nineteenth-century ironstone miners around Hutton-le-Hole were hard drinkers and tremendous scrappers, renowned for hard living with plenty of knocks, far removed from Parliamentary commissioners and investigative journalists.

Female harrier in belt and chain. (courtesy National Coal Mining Museum, Wakefield)

Fishing apprentices

Almost impossible to monitor was the plight of hapless fishing apprentices from Hull and the coastal areas. Young boys taken on from workhouses had few protectors on the fishing smacks where much gratuitous brutality had to be endured. Some would have graduated from the ragged and industrial school in Mill Street which from 1868 supported a training ship, the *Southampton*. Here, orphaned and delinquent lads learned knotting, splicing, seamanship and a smattering of reading and arithmetic. 'Decky learners' became men overnight. When the vessels docked there were often desertions and imprisonments.

A particular case in 1881 was that of William Papper, fourteen-year-old apprentice on the smack *Rising Sun*. Repeatedly and savagely beaten, he was thrown into bilge water, trampled on and deliberately starved by the skipper, Osmann Otto Brand. Eventually the boy was so badly assaulted, that he could not be revived.

Although few shipmates came to his aid at the time, witnesses at the Leeds Assizes confirmed the inhumane treatment. After due trial, Brand was hanged at Armley on 23 May 1882. The incident led to a Board of Trade inquiry. Some critics felt that the subsequent report favoured owners and captains, and irregular punishments continued.

Hard home lessons

In rural areas like the East Riding, many lads from the age of thirteen were hired out to work on farms. As 'Tommy Owt' novices, doing any kind of odd job demanded of them, they learned to fit in, gradually learning their skills as ploughmen. Removed from home, they suffered much ritual bullying, especially by wagoners-in-charge, who might administer kicks, or punches, pushing heads under a horse's tail or holding a victim under a pump.

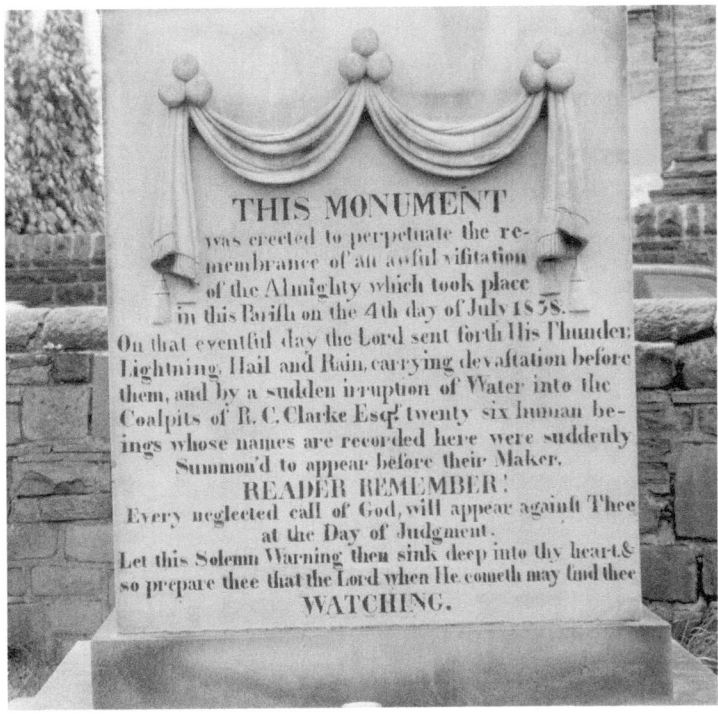

Silkstone monument.

Silkstone monument.

Girls in service suffered many privations, sanctions and abuse. Emma Martin of Castleford, a twelve-year-old servant wrote in 1891:

> I polish and wash and clean and scrub. Once a week I have to scrub the lavatory. I have to scrub the wooden top, whitewash the sides and scrub the floor. God help me if it's not spotless… there's loads of ironing to do and the iron seems to get heavier and heavier. God help me if I burn anything.

Sexual abuse was rarely discussed. Pauper girls were especially at risk. Child prostitution in the Yorkshire towns was a social problem, unalleviated by gestures such as raising the age of consent from thirteen to sixteen in 1885.

The age of criminal responsibility – seven since the eighteenth century – so often seemed to be on the law's blindside. Little account was taken of a delinquent's home background. Children were punished like adults. Their cause was taken up by Benjamin Waugh, Settle's most famous son, born there in 1838. A Congregationalist minister, he saw many child offenders as victims of neglect who needed help. His book, *The Gaol-Cradle – Who rocks it?* (1873) was a plea for the abolition of much juvenile punishment. Places were found for many child vagrants in regular employment, including the Army and Navy. In 1884 he founded the National Society for the Prevention of Cruelty to Children. By 1886 the Hull branch lodged some 478 children at its shelter in Sykes Street.

By the closing years of Queen Victoria's reign public opinion was coming to recognise childhood as a developmental phase on the way to adult responsibilities. During her eight years on the Bradford Board of Education (starting in 1894), Margaret McMillan won many battles for deprived children. She persuaded the authority to provide baths: the Wapping Street School Baths were the nation's first. Nursery schools, medical inspections and free school meals for necessitous children followed.

Our modern conscience is disturbed by news of child abuse. We may begin to accept that some past ill-use may have been caused by over-rigorous adults, as in the ancient jest – 'All new babbies i' Oxenthorpe has their bums smacked wi' a bank book!' It often turns out to be true that today's bullied waif becomes tomorrow's incorrigible thug. Ebenezer Elliott, the Corn Law Rhymer, champion of the underdog, commented thus on certain Sheffield youth before the Children's Employment Commission, 1843: 'The horrid words of these incipient sages and legislators; their ferocious gestures; their hideous laughter; their brutal, bloated, mindless faces appal and amaze the stranger.'

Rammalations

Mention of Rammalations, or 'Beating the Bounds', enables this chapter to end on a lighter note. Every few years at Rogationtide, just before Ascension Day, villagers might gather to assert their historic rights to walk their boundaries, and to initiate youngsters into the importance of maintaining such salient features as streams, pathways, hedgerows and the like. Often a particular 'bound' would be emphasised by horseplay – pushing a child into a ditch, or lightly bouncing him on a boulder. These extended walks called for adequate refreshment. Between 1816 and 1823 the bill for liquor at Harrogate's Black Swan increased to £2 6s – a rise of 64 per cent!

From early days children are conditioned by home and neighbourhood attitudes. If they live with violence, anti-social behaviour and unreasonable punishment, they, in turn, are likely to adopt similar standards. The drift into crime becomes foreseeable, perhaps inevitable. All of which raises again the question – is it punishment that will reform and deter?

The Revd Benjamin Waugh. (courtesy National Society for the Prevention of Cruelty to Children)

chapter eight

Royal Reckonings

Harrying the North

Even when his Conquest looked complete, William the Conqueror had trouble in Yorkshire. In 1068 two Saxon earls, Edwin and Morcar, betrayed his trust, and York had to be subdued. The slaughter of a Norman force in Durham, followed by an incursion of Danish raiders which overpowered York, called forth other expeditions to restore order. Several sieges of the town's wooden castles had to be relieved, including one where the royal sheriff, William de Malet, had to appeal for help.

Once more the King returned, vowing vengeance 'by the splendour of God' to root out Northumbria (ie Yorkshire) to the Scottish borders, in an unforgettable coup. Ruthless genocide followed, with butchery on an epic scale. Village by village was put to the sword, with the corpses of men, women and children left to putrefy where they fell. Crops, corn and equipment were burnt. Little was spared, save isolated buildings like St John of Beverley's church. According to the historian Simon of Durham, 'There was no village inhabited between York and Durham. They became lurking places to wild beasts and robber and were a great dread to travellers'. Wolves and wild dogs cleaned the bones of the fallen.

For refugees the winter of 1069 brought famine and disease. The Bishop of Durham fled to Lindisfarne, taking with him the sacred dust of Cuthbert. As far as the River Tees, the countryside was laid waste. William, having been crowned at York, and spending Christmas there, turned his ferocious soldiery south-west to Chester. Tradition has it that he lost an advance party in moorland snowstorms, despite heroic efforts to find them. Did expressions like 'swearing like Bill the Norman' and 'cussing like Billio' really originate here? It is a fanciful thought.

For decades much of the land remained barren, and recovery was slow. Near Bradfield (WR), for example, the manors of Ughill, Worall and Wadsley were regarded as 'waste' for over a century. In William's Domesday Book, drawn up as a national inventory in 1086, it was claimed that hundreds of former Yorkshire settlements were without a single inhabitant. While there are many allusions to 'waste', interpretation is difficult, especially 1,000 years on. Other social and economic factors may well have operated. In the Dales and western fringes William's depredations were less thorough, some families, having exploited the land agriculturally, simply moved on to fresher pastures.

Finally, the King elevated strong men to strategic commands. Fortresses were built at key places like Skipton, where Robert de Romill held strict court. Ilbert de Lacy exercised a repressive presence at Pontefract. Ironically for the later Norman rulers, trouble flared continuously from another quarter – Scotland, the source of many determined raids during the thirteenth and fourteenth centuries.

For many years the Anglo-Saxons were mistrusted, and even in spiritual affairs, archbishops continued to be Norman churchmen; the See of York was subordinated to Canterbury.

On his deathbed William apparently repented of his savagery in Yorkshire. His 'scorched earth' reprisals went deep into folk psyche, and – who knows? – his harrying may help to explain our residual doubts regarding owt at's foreign!

Castles built by the Normans to suppress local insurrection became ideal for holding royal prisoners. At various times Richmond held three Kings: William, the Lion of Scotland, pending a ransom after his capture at Alnwick in 1174; David II of Scotland after his defeat at Neville's Cross, 1346; and Charles I in 1647, whilst en route to Northampton.

During the Wars of the Roses, Edward IV was held for a time (1466) in Middleham Castle, by Richard Neville, Earl of Warwick (the Kingmaker), Edward having shown the temerity to wed a Woodville instead of a Neville. After Warwick's defeat at Barnet in 1471, Edward gave the castle to the future Richard III. This ill-famed monarch imprisoned in Sheriff Hutton castle his nephew Edward Plantagenet, and his great-niece, Elizabeth of York, who feared a proposal of marriage from her captor!

'Bloody Pomfret'

Pontefract Castle has several punitive royal connections. Thomas of Lancaster was beheaded opposite the castle on Tattersall ridge in 1322, after the failure of his rebellion against Edward II (his uncle), and defeat at Boroughbridge. The Duc d'Orleans was imprisoned with other nobles after defeat at Agincourt in 1415. And there had been the sad demise of Richard II.

The only son of Edward the Black Prince, and grandson of Edward III, whom he succeeded in 1377 at the age of ten, Richard lived in turbulent times. His realm was exhausted by wars in France and wearied by Scottish invasions. Hopeful of finding a remedy, his Parliament imposed a poll tax in 1380 which incited a serious and widespread revolt of the peasantry. Sympathetic at first, the young King promised to help the poorest of his subjects, but soon changed his mind.

He had plenty of other problems. The landed lords mistrusted his stance over the peasants. The church was opposed to his defence of the Lollards, the heretical followers of Yorkshire-born John Wycliff. Many nobles were critical of his peace policy towards France, in which, however, the King persisted. And, as always, there was trouble in Ireland. His position seemed more secure after he stood up to his nobles: Gloucester died in a Calais jail; Arundel was beheaded; Warwick was imprisoned.

Biding his time was a deadlier opponent – and potential rival – his cousin, Henry Bolingbroke, son of John of Gaunt of the House of Lancaster. When a quarrel broke out between Bolingbroke and Thomas Mowbray, Duke of Norfolk, the Commons decided that the matter should be decided by single combat. At the last moment Richard intervened, banishing Mowbray for life and Bolingbroke for ten years, depriving him of his inheritance.

Timely self-assertion was one thing: arbitrary royal decree was another. The King's claim to divine right could not protect him from criticism when, for example, he tried to extort loans. Not only did he misjudge his prerogative and the continuing loyalty of his supporters – he chose to leave for Ireland where the Earl of March had just been killed.

A few weeks later in August 1399 Bolingbroke landed at Ravenspur (Spurn) to reclaim his father's estates – and more, if circumstances favoured. Henry Percy, Earl of Northumberland and other northern grandees rallied, and Richard, recalled from Ireland, was obliged to meet Bolingbroke at Flint Castle. He was arrested and lodged in the Tower of London, having no choice but to acknowledge his cousin as Duke of Lancaster, and then abdicate. It was a foregone conclusion that the assembled lords and commons would accept the usurper, and so arose the House of Lancaster under King Henry IV.

The violent death of a King.

Richard II.

The deposed monarch was despatched to Yorkshire, spending a few nights at Knaresborough Castle, before being escorted to Pontefract. Exactly how Richard died is uncertain, but the circumstances were suspicious. He may have starved himself to death, or was simply left to die. Rumours later abounded, one telling of sleep deprivation and torture by constant drum beats. According to Shakespeare, he was cruelly butchered by Sir Piers Exton.

On the brink of his own execution the deed was recalled by Earl Rivers:

> O Pomfret, Pomfret! O thou bloody prison,
> Fatal and ominous to noble peers!
> Within the guilty closure of thy walls
> Richard the Second here was hack'd to death;
> And, for more slander to thy dismal seat,
> We give to thee our guiltless blood to drink'. (*King Richard III*, III 3)

Tradition has it that the corpse was originally interred at King's Langley, Hertfordshire before removal to Westminster Abbey. Richard le Scrope, his chancellor, who began the building of Bolton Castle in 1379, donated to Easby Abbey funds for six priests quartered at Bolton to pray daily for the soul of Richard II.

Suppression of the monasteries

For Henry VIII any satisfaction arising from his title, Defender of the Faith, bequeathed by Pope Leo X, was short-lived. He wanted to consolidate himself as supreme head of the Church of England, to marry Anne Boleyn – having rejected his Catholic consort, Catherine of Aragon – and to take over the immense wealth of the Church. Back in 1521 his Archbishop of York and Lord Chancellor, Cardinal Wolsey had expressed concern about monastic worldliness, foreign allegiances and revenues lost to Rome. Officials of the new royal counsellor and vicar-general, Thomas Cromwell, found ignorance, licence, the wearing of unseemly fashionable garments and neglect. At Rievaulx the abbot had taken over the infirmary for lavish entertainment. At Kirkbymoorside Priory there had been waywardness and breaches of discipline. Numbers generally had fallen. Fountains Abbey was reduced to thirty-two monks, Bolton Abbey fifteen.

Accordingly, Henry had ammunition to justify sanctions. The smaller houses with an income of less than £200 were to go first, their property diverted to the Crown, and monks and nuns pensioned off.

Local murmurings spread from Lincolnshire to East Yorkshire, where protesters organised a 'Pilgrimage of Grace', parading banners emblazoned with the five wounds of Christ. Robert Aske of Aughton gained support as far west as Halifax. Abbots and priors lent varying degrees of support, although Archbishop Lee of York was rough-handled for condemning the insurgents. After the pilgrims had won over Hull and Doncaster, the Duke of Norfolk, instructed by an infuriated monarch, parleyed with a rebel committee, and there was a partial stand-down in the hope of saving the monasteries.

But for Henry the protest was treason: 'You must cause such dreadful execution upon a good number of the inhabitants,' he ordered Norfolk, 'hanging them in towns, quartering them and setting their heads and quarters in every town as shall be a fearful warning' – words reminiscent of William the Conqueror's orders to his army in Harrying the North.

Prominent among those who paid the full price were several monastic heads. Adam Sedbergh, Abbot of Jervaulx, had been intimidated and placed in an impossible position. Fearful of the

Badge of the Pilgrimage of Grace.

outcome of armed resistance to the King, he had baulked at supporting the rebels, who had jostled him, fleeing to hide on Witton Fell for four days before returning to oppose the rising. Reviled as a traitor, he was given the choice of joining or beheading. He joined – only to be hanged eventually in York. So was Abbot Thirsk of Fountains, forced to resign on charges of sacrilege and theft, and arrested for complicity in the Pilgrimage. And so was William Wood, Prior of Bridlington who also had been drawn in by threats when the bailiffs of Kilham and Nafferton vowed to behead him if he refused to send helpers. He made the mistake of recruiting eleven mounted retainers.

Secular leaders could expect no mercy. On 12 July 1537, a market day, Robert Aske was paraded through the streets on a hurdle, hanged and then beheaded on York Pavement, and his corpse hung in chains from Clifford's Tower. Sir Robert Constable, hanged over Hull's Beverley Gate, was still gibbeted there four years later when Henry VIII returned to inspect the fortifications. Thomas, Lord Darcy, high steward of Selby Abbey had his estates near Temple Newsam confiscated and he too was beheaded at Tower Hill.

In 1539 there began the dissolution of the larger monasteries. Fountains Abbey, initially sold to Sir Richard Gresham, had by the end of the century passed to Sir Stephen Proctor, who used the infirmary as a quarry for the building of Fountains Hall. From the Benedictine Abbey of St Mary's, York stone was removed to repair the Ouse Bridge, and in the early eighteenth century to bolster St Olave's church and Beverley Minster.

The buildings were systematically looted. Lead was removed from the vast roofs, and bells were sold. Crosses, chalices, candlesticks, hangings and vestments enriched the wives of the spoilers. Grain, livestock and wool disappeared. A few artefacts were rescued like the rood screen, carried by twenty men, according to tradition, from Jervaulx, and refitted on the south side of the chancel in St Andrew's church, Aysgarth. From Easby Abbey an oak screen graces Wensley church, and some of the bells and stalls with misericords were transported to St Mary's church, Richmond.

Part of the Bridlington Priory church tapestry.

There were incalculable losses – in local industry, technology, agriculture, estate management, medicine, shelter and care. Poverty was made so much worse as itinerants lost their accustomed lodgings. Monastic scholarship disappeared. Libraries of sacred texts were looted or lost. At Fountains, priceless manuscripts were sold cheaply. Henry's dissolution can be seen as, in part, political retribution on a national scale. Since the monastic empire amounted to approximately a quarter of all England, Yorkshire's dominance brought a proportionate loss and dislocation.

The ruins of many architectural wonders, melancholy or romantic, in beautiful settings, have bequeathed to us a remarkable legacy of grandeur and nobility.

Mary, Queen of Scots

In 1558, at sixteen, Mary married the French Dauphin, Francis, soon becoming Queen on her father-in-law's death. Within a year she was a widow. Returning to Scotland, she made no secret of her designs on the throne of England, occupied by Elizabeth, daughter of Henry VIII and Anne Boleyn, whose marriage, in Catholic eyes, was invalid.

Mary was caught up in a chaotic sequence of events. In 1566 her talented and attentive Italian secretary, David Riccio, was stabbed to death by her jealous husband, Lord Darnley. The following year he, in turn, was strangled on the orders of the Earl of Rothwell, possibly with Mary's connivance. But her realm was scandalised when within three months she wed Rothwell. When the Protestant nobility moved to depose her, Mary appealed to Elizabeth for help, having

Mary, Queen of Scots. (courtesy of the Marquess of Salisbury)

Bolton Castle.

been forced to abdicate in favour of her infant son James. She arrived at Workington on 16 May 1568, never to return to Scotland.

Elizabeth was deeply uncertain what to do. To return her cousin to Scotland would be to condemn her outright. But to pass her on to Catholic France or Spain might induce her to put herself at the head of a foreign army. Then again, as a great-niece of Henry VIII she had some claim to the throne of England…

Initially Mary was placed in the care of Lord Scrope, governor of Carlisle Castle. But further orders from Elizabeth brought a transfer to Bolton Castle, built in 1379 for Richard II's chancellor, Richard le Scrope, where she was to be held in 'honourable custody'. She was welcomed to Bolton by Sir Henry and Lady Scrope on 15 July, and given a suite in the south-west tower, with glorious views over Wensleydale.

Some of her forty retainers had to be billeted in the village. Here, unmoved by the scenery, she spent six melancholy months, closely guarded by Sir Francis Knollys, her 'good scholemaster' who had been with her at Carlisle, and endeavoured to add English to her ready command of Latin, French and the Gaelic.

Every effort was made towards her regal accommodation. She liked her hair coiffured regularly, and as a skilled needlewoman she applied herself to tapestries and embroideries. Breviary in hand, she paced her apartments. Everywhere she was watched, especially on hunting expeditions. Rumours grew of an intrigue with the Duke of Norfolk, brother of Lord Scrope. Time was spent, too, in penning letters to influential people who might reopen her case with the Queen.

On one occasion, accompanied by her lively young friend Kit Norton, she threw off her guards, only to be overtaken at Queen's Gap on Leyburn Shawl (where, says tradition, she dropped a shawl), only a short distance from the market place. Thereafter a dozen men rode

Plaque, Ripon market place.

with her on all outings. As guest of Sir Christopher Metcalfe she also stayed at Nappa Hall near Askrigg, where later generations have claimed to see her ghost. On 26 January 1569 she was moved on to Tutbury, via Ripon.

During the eighteen years of her wandering captivity there were regular fears of Catholic plots in her support. An early and serious event was in November 1569 with the rise of the northern earls, led by Percy of Northumberland and Neville of Westmoreland. The rebels celebrated mass in Durham and Ripon cathedrals, and Protestant prayer books were burnt, but loyalty to Elizabeth was proclaimed and the spirit of the protest seemed more symbolically religious than political. There was no question of revolution. Northumberland, having fled to Scotland, was sold back for £2,000 and beheaded without trial on York Pavement on 22 August 1572. His head was spiked on Micklegate Bar. Hundreds of followers were hanged.

In 1574 Mary was restored to Yorkshire, interned at Sheffield Manor in the Turret House, which still survives. It may have been purpose-built for her accommodation, later becoming a hunting lodge for George Talbot, Earl of Shrewsbury. Here and at Sheffield Castle the 6th earl and his notorious wife, Bess of Hardwick were in charge of Mary for some fourteen years. Her attendants were forbidden to carry swords, bows or shafts. Special permission was needed for her to leave the premises. Elizabeth demanded regular reassurances that her rival could not escape.

Mary always longed for more understanding. She kept up her needlework. Her beauty and manners fascinated her attendants and carefully screened visitors, but the sadness of captivity and inertia made her pine. As her health suffered she was allowed to visit Buxton in the autumn of 1575, thanks to the mediation of the French ambassador. She took the waters and visited Chatsworth. In 1580 on a subsequent visit she fell from her horse, injuring her back; for some time she had to be carried about, and became sickly for want of exercise.

On 3 March 1584 she left Sheffield Castle for South Wingfield, Derbyshire. Anthony Babington, a page at Sheffield, remained a devoted follower, acting as intermediary with friends on the continent. In 1586 he was involved in a plot resulting in an insurrection to free Mary and murder Elizabeth and some of her ministers. Letters exchanged between Babington and Mary were intercepted and her conspirator was seized and executed.

Turret House, Sheffield.

Mary Queen of Scots: exhibiton, Bolton Castle.

Elizabeth now accepted the inevitable. In the great hall of Fotheringham Castle, Northamptonshire, Mary was put on trial, convicted – and reluctantly the Queen signed the necessary warrant. Mary met her death with characteristic courage and dignity. The axe fell on 8 February 1587.

Charles I

On 23 April, 1642 Sir John Hotham had the misfortune, as governor of Hull, but acting on Parliamentary orders, to have to raise the drawbridge of Hull's Beverley Gate in order to keep out Charles I, ostensibly calling to see his son, the Duke of York – but also to check on the Parliamentary arsenal.

After waiting for some hours, the King was obliged to return to Beverley. Much later Sir John changed sides, but was caught after escaping Parliamentary troops just north of Beverley, and escorted to Hull. He was beheaded on 2 January 1645, the day after his son, Captain John, had been executed on a similar charge of treason. Royal pride was no doubt satisfied.

But life – and death – confers many punitive ironies, even for royalty. Charles's Queen, Henrietta Maria, sailing from Holland in February 1643 to mobilise funds and military support, was forced by a storm into Bridlington Bay. When a house where she took shelter was threatened by a Parliamentary naval bombardment, she found hasty refuge in a ditch – an ignoble plight indeed. She did, however, eventually reach sanctuary in York.

Following the Civil War, Charles was held as a prisoner in Porch House, Northallerton, 1647 – where, seven years earlier, he had been a most honoured guest. And, of course, his turn at the scaffold was yet to come.

Sir John Hotham, governor of Hull.

Above: Charles I locked out at Hull's Beverley Gate. Based on painting by Joseph Parrocel. (courtesy of Hull Museums)

Right: Porch House, Northallerton.

chapter nine

Changing Attitudes

The causes of crime cannot be reduced to a simplistic context of poverty, fecklessness and greed – though these seemingly constant factors are not to be underrated. Victorian paternalists like Sir Titus Salt had well understood that much crime was drink related, hence his refusal to provide a pub in Saltaire – 'no pub, no pawn shop, no police station'. Among the Yorkshire clergymen who actively appreciated the links between deprivation and crime was John Hymers, rector of Brandesburton (1852-87), whose will was to establish Hymers College, Hull; and who, as a magistrate, often paid the fines of those he felt sorry for. As vicar of Helmsley from 1870 to 1913, Charles Norris Gray preached and practised a welfare policy of decent housing, clean water supply, good food and proper clothing. Workhouse children, he argued, earned more self-respect in their own clothes rather than a drab uniform, which drew attention to their lowly status.

At the turn of the twentieth century Seebohm Rowntree found that over a quarter of the citizens of York were living in poverty. Subsequent findings down to our own time have confirmed that the roots of crime are often embedded in low moral understanding, inadequate homes, lack of education and opportunity, and rejection leading to social deviance. Particularly at risk was every rising generation surrounded by unsatisfactory role models such as absent fathers.

From such backgrounds it has long been apparent that young male offenders present a special challenge to law and order. Up to the nineteenth century, youth was widely regarded as a dangerous phase, with a need for curbs and controls. Recidivism loomed larger when lads went home from reformatories and industrial schools, though these institutions were deemed successful in acting as buffers between youngsters and hardened prisoners. Positive outside support was needed. In 1876 a start was made with the 'missionaries and mentors' sponsored by the Church of England Temperance Society, active in the West Riding towns to arrange release on bail, a forerunner of probation. To set this system on a national basis was a logical step; and the Probation of Offenders Act (1907) established professional supervision within the local community.

With the Children and Young Persons Act (1933) the age of criminal responsibility was raised to eight. A 'child' became a 'young person' at fourteen; and welfare and re-education were stressed, allowing agencies like local authorities and the NSPCC to bring straying youngsters to court for care and protection. During the 1930s reformatories and industrial schools were renamed 'approved schools', where a three-year sentence was standard, but good behaviour could bring earlier release. Parents were to be involved in counselling. Punishments included withdrawal of privileges, periods of isolation and up to twelve strokes of the cane on the buttocks. From 1969 approved schools were redesignated community homes.

Birching for young persons (in practice, boys only) was abolished under the Criminal Justice Act (1948) which introduced an alternative favoured in right-wing circles and revived at intervals – the detention centre, transmuted into young offender institutions by the 1980s. One of the first experimental centres was set up at the Marfleet Lane Remand Home, Hull. This was the 'short, sharp shock', with inmates subjected to barrack-type accommodation, with quasi-military discipline and a brisk physical regime. Closely cropped hair, abolished in the 1920s was restored, as were solitary confinement and dietary sanctions. The results, however, have been ambivalent. Many of the trainees seemed to thrive on the system, raising doubts as to its deterrent value. For girls the regime proved unsuitable and was abandoned.

On the home front the turmoil of the Second World War created immense family strains, many fathers having been absent for some years during formative periods of their children's upbringing. With international peace the crime rates, especially burglary, moved up noticeably, nearly half the offenders being under seventeen. In 1958 the chief constable for Hull remarked in his annual report:

> To find the figures rising at such an alarming rate despite all the attention lavished on youth by official and voluntary organisations and the work of experts in the care and reform of delinquents is extremely disturbing and disappointing.

Alas, the sixties was the era of mods and rockers, with skirmishes at Bridlington and Scarborough. Skinheads stalked the streets in the seventies; and in the eighties soccer violence flared in Leeds and Sheffield, not all of it caused by visiting fans. Authority was flouted, and turbulent youth fomented social disorder on a scale not seen since the nineteenth century and the prison population rose.

But prison, it seemed, neither deterred nor reformed – a view urged by the Departmental Committee on Prisons, 1895, by Home Secretary Herbert Asquith – a Yorkshireman born at Morley. The committee recommended looking to the causes of crime and to rehabilitation, which, together with 'therapeutic incarceration', might strengthen the criminal character towards more law-abiding ways. From 1919 warders became prison officers, exercising more of a pastoral and welfare role. More visiting time was allowed. Prisoners were allowed to eat with their fellows. Voluntary teachers were recruited to provide basic education. Further signs of a more liberal regime came in 1948 with the abolition of penal servitude, or hard labour like stone-breaking. Flogging, rarely used after mid-century, was abolished in 1967.

Despite the adverse publicity when trust was betrayed, there was some success with open prisons. Newhall Wood, near Wakefield, opened in 1934 was the first to pioneer new approaches, taking inmates from the local jail for the last stage of their sentence. The farm still operates. In 1946 Askham Grange near York was opened to cater for about 100 women in the last year of their sentences.

Still numbers rose. A massaging device was the suspended sentence introduced through the 1967 Criminal Justice Act, delaying a prison sentence for up to two years on condition of good behaviour. A concurrent feature was parole, offering release on licence for those who had served twelve months or one-third of the sentence, whichever was the greater. A recent extension of the parole principle is the 'home detention curfew', typically 7 a.m. to 7 p.m., with electronic tagging.

For many years reports by successive chief inspectors of prisons had condemned the degrading lavatorial practice of 'slopping out'. Various surveys, including the Woolf Report on Prison Disturbances, 1990, showed that inmates would rather have access to proper lavatory facilities than the resolution of other problems, such as overcrowding. During the last decade of the millennium this offensive routine was phased out.

Nevertheless, prison remains an ultimate sanction and hopefully a deterrent for some. Sheer numbers have meant that many inmates are 'banged up' for much of the day, drastically reducing the time available for recreation and education. Bullying has been highlighted as a serious issue, not least in some Yorkshire prisons where a number of suicides have brought media attention. The Howard League for Penal Reform has consistently argued that too many offenders are sent to prison, and that more institutions multiply the scale of the problems – again, a view resonant in Yorkshire with a rash of penal institutions in the Doncaster area: HMP Lindholme, together with Young Offender Institutions at Moorland, Marshgate and Hatfield; while near York is Full Sutton (maximum security, 1989); and, experimentally, at South Cave, alongside HMP Everthorpe is the Wolds Prison, the first of its kind to be contracted out to a private company. Another concern of the Howard League is the unacceptably large numbers of mentally disturbed prisoners in need of proper professional care.

Treatment rather than prison for certain kinds of drug offenders has been recommended by the National Association for the Resettlement of Offenders. It is ironic that drug trafficking within prisons perpetuates and compounds the problem. The association continues to point to the inherent difficulties of preparing offenders for rehabilitation whilst in captivity. The fact that half of all prisoners released have no proper homes to return to underlines basic domestic welfare shortcomings. So much has been done to ameliorate the lot of the prisoner – but some aspects of their environment are not too dissimilar to those railed against by Victorian reformers.

Further to public disquiet over particular miscarriages of justice, as with Timothy Evans, posthumously pardoned in 1966, the abolition of the death penalty in 1969 brought to the fore that category of prisoners known as 'lifers'. While some cases are reviewed after ten or fifteen years, others involved such horrific circumstances that 'life' had to mean permanent custody. The outstanding case, of course, was Peter Sutcliffe, the Yorkshire Ripper. who from 1975 terrorised the West Riding for six years. Born in Bingley in 1946, Sutcliffe murdered thirteen women, receiving a life sentence on each account, and attempted seven others. At the Old Bailey in May 1981 Mr Justice Boreham declared that a minimum of thirty years should be served. The Ripper's inner compulsions – voices from God urging him to murder prostitutes – had been unsuspected by his family, his lorry-driving colleagues or police – who nevertheless interviewed him eight times as a possible suspect before a routine inquiry on his car registration led to his arrest. Instead of being committed to a secure psychiatric hospital, Sutcliffe was at first sent to HMP Parkhurst.

Life sentence plans as at Wakefield, the county's main lifer institution, continuously assesses prisoners' attitudes to authority, the victims, behaviour problems etc. Prison officers and psychiatrists have to consider most carefully in what supervised circumstances the longer-term inmate will be released. Stringent risk assessment will continue to be made in considering early release and rehabilitation... but mistakes are bound to occur, given the vagaries – and unpredictability – of human nature.

Our modern hierarchy of punishments can be summarised as follows:-

- A police caution.
- Conditional discharge.
- Binding over for good behaviour (with origins in the Justice of the Peace Act, 1361).
- Probation.
- Community service – a recurring theme endorsed by the 1991 Criminal Justice Act, emphasising reparation rather than punishment.
- Combination order – community service with probation.
- Curfew order: the 1998 Anti-Social Behaviour Order domiciling an offender up to twelve hours a day, for up to six months. Acceptable Behaviour Contracts, also with parental involvement, are aimed at youthful offenders.

- Suspended sentence.
- Prison, a last resort, not least because it is perceived as a training ground for further crime.

Fines, of course, could be imposed at various points in the system, depending on circumstances.

Calls for the return of stocks and pillory are unlikely to be heeded; and ducking stools are not going to reappear on the banks of Swale or Don. Humiliation, retribution and repression have not brought the success commensurate with public expectations, and physical constraints are largely confined to the curfew and imprisonment.

Making the punishment fit the crime once seemed logical, even reasonable; but individual circumstances vary, and courts have used discretion over factors like past record, parental attitudes and support, aggression and contrition. Young delinquents, especially, have been portrayed as victims of environment not of their own making – a paradoxical situation which gains credence by contact with some of our urban high-rise estates, where, through many an evening and well into the night, youngsters unaccompanied, unchecked and unpoliced, roam at will.

If these areas are not to continue as breeding grounds for anti-social and criminal induction, parental awareness has to be aroused, and social morale has obvious environmental determinants. Play areas and social centres for young people need to be integral to new housing plans. Revitalised streets and a return to community values will tend to reduce crime and vandalism. Optimism is good for us all but there is no easy slide-rule cause-and-effect relationship between environment and crime. Sadly, some 'lifers' are inevitable. The Old Adam lurks in many of us. Greed, envy, lust, vanity, revenge, temptation motivate apparently respectable citizens to break the law. What chance then for youngsters from bad homes, where flouting authority and intimidation are the norm; where punishment is an accepted risk of the calling and where elders seem to glory in their criminal reputations and where a prison background confers prestige?

Close-circuit television to monitor and deter in city streets tend to divert the problems elsewhere. Extra urban vigilance causes criminals to migrate to the countryside. As long ago as 1836 the Leeds Watch Committee received complaints from the (then) village of Headingly of such a trend. New ideas often turn out to be old ones revisited. Neighbourhood Watch has some echoes of frankpledge!

How to reclaim criminals is an abiding question. As Mr Justice Firth, well experienced in Yorkshire, has recently observed, 'The decisive question is whether the offender wants to go straight'. Getting and keeping a job may provide a motivation hitherto missing. Clearly there is a need for more education and job training for prisoners, many of whom have been poorly educated. Better schooling could save many a sentence!

No, crime is not likely to disappear from our Broad Acres, but hopefully it can be better contained. It will be interesting to see, as this new millennium advances, what permutations of old and new penalties will be tried. Extensions of the principle of reparation and community service look likely, together with schemes of re-education and rehabilitation with special provision for such categories of offenders as drug takers and the mentally disturbed; and well, yes, prison....

In 100 years time – who knows? – some of our hopeful and sophisticated sanctions, continuously updated, may be patronisingly dismissed as Olde Yorkshire Punishments!

Select Bibliography

Andrews A., *Old Time Punishments* (Tabard Press: 1970)

Benson G., *York Assizes* (York Castle Museum: 1920)

Campling E., *The Police* (Dryad Press: 1989)

Cawthorne N., *The Strange Laws of Old England* (Piatkus Books: 2004)

Duncan R.S., *The West Riding House of Correction* (H.M. Prison, Wakefield: 1995)

Forster G.C.F., *The East Riding Justices of the Peace in the Seventeenth Century* (East Riding Local History society: 1973)

Howorth P., *Crimes and Punishments in Yorkshire 1800-1837* (Lowndes Publications: 1993)

Kelly T., *HMP Leeds: 150 years – A Brief History* (1997)

Longley K., *Ecclesiastical Cause Papers at York: Dean and Chapter's Court, 1350 –1843* (Borthwick Text: 1890)

Newbery E. & Wood T., *Punishment and Prisons* (Galleries of Justice, Nottingham: 1996)

Rose L., *Crime and Punishment* (Batsford: 1977)

Sharpe J.A., *Judicial Punishment in England* (Faber & Faber: 1990)

Spence D., *Crime and Punishment* (Addax Retail Publishing: 1995)

Sterling J., *Famous Northern Crimes, Trials and Criminals* (Hesketh, Ormskirk: 1983)

Turner J.H., *Annals of Wakefield House of Correction* (1904)

Viner C., *Police in Britain* (Ripon Museum Trust: 1984)

Walker P., *Punishment: An Illustrated History* (David & Charles: 1972)

First published in 2008 by The History Press

Reprinted 2008, 2010, 2012

The History Press
The Mill, Brimscombe Port,
Stroud, Gloucestershire, GL5 2QG
www.thehistorypress.co.uk

© Howard Peach, 2008

The right of Howard Peach to be identified as the Author
of this work has been asserted in accordance with the
Copyrights, Designs and Patents Act 1988.

All rights reserved. No part of this book may be reprinted
or reproduced or utilised in any form or by any electronic,
mechanical or other means, now known or hereafter invented,
including photocopying and recording, or in any information
storage or retrieval system, without the permission in writing
from the Publishers.

British Library Cataloguing in Publication Data.
A catalogue record for this book is available from the British Library.

ISBN 978 0 7524 4661 5

Typesetting and origination by The History Press.
Printed in Great Britain